In the Shadows of the Ancestors

A Journey Through Africa and Into the Self

HASSAN ANSAH

Printed in the United States of America

First Printing, 2016

ISBN: 978-0-9978327-0-9

IRIN Publishing

New York, Geneva, Nairobi

www.irinnews.org

Everything that we see is a shadow cast by that which we do not see.
Dr. Martin Luther King Jr.

I will not try to relay a special philosophy, political ideology, or moral point of view; I will simply tell the truth about my experiences as an Afro-American journalist living and working on the African continent. I will summarize my preconceived notions, as well as my newfound perspectives on Sub-Saharan African culture, and to the best of my abilities show how the two mesh and synchronize interdependently, and reflect them back in my unique narrative. It is my belief that life is a kaleidoscope that offers a myriad of different ways of looking at reality. This book is my way of analyzing, assessing, and emerging into an entirely different world, which I was exposed to. My goal is to unfold; to describe Africa with authenticity without becoming another addition to the athenaeum of negative despondency and to shed some light on the profound intricacies that make up the myriad of cultures known as Sub-Saharan Africa both internally and externally.

Along this journey, I experienced the good, the bad, the ugly, and ultimately the real! There were many memorable, interesting, noble, hardworking, treacherous, ruthless, dedicated, and most of all, human characters that I met along the way. The characters in my book are as diverse as Africa is itself. From the large Hindu population of Nairobi, Kenya, to the Nilotic Nubian Minorities of Upper Egypt, all the different communities that I came into contact with left an indelible mark on my growth and experience as both a writer and a human being. While reading this book, one may wonder why I choose to call myself Afro-American as opposed to African-American. This is a personal choice that reflects my unique understanding of a cultural and historical connection and also disconnection that many Americans of African descent feel when returning to the land of our ancestors. To me, the prefix Afro- denotes a derivative coming from a particular source. Using Afro-American for me has the same emblematic relationship as a branch growing out from the root of a tree.

The African cultural construct allowed a transplanted people to gain a sense of durability and purpose. These cultural branches helped to explain the invisible and imperceptible, and thus allowed the transfiguration of a throng of disparate people into a coherent social group with a strong sense of history and continuity. By relying on hybrid African commonalities and shared, yet diverse, cultural expressions, we remodeled and restored our reality.

From the sandy beaches of Jamaica to the concrete brownstones of Harlem, Africa shines her light through many distinct expressions. One clear-cut example of this would be the Rastafarian movement.

The Rastafarian movement started in Jamaica during the '30s following a prophecy that was given by the black nationalist leader Marcus Garvey. The Rastafarian philosophical history began with the colonization of Africa, better known as "Ethiopia," by Europeans. Wherever enslaved Africans were taken and dispersed throughout the world became known to a Rastafari as "Babylon." For the Rastafarian, this exile showed the oppression of their culture. They believed that freedom and liberty would only come once all blacks returned to Ethiopia. Marcus Garvey urged blacks to "Look to Africa where a black king shall be crowned; he will be a liberator." This statement became the very essence of the Rastafarian movement. Along with its unique vegetarian diet and reggae musical expressions, these distinct cultural expressions could only have grown out of the unique Afro-Jamaican consciousness. The root of the tree, "Africa," allowed the diaspora to restructure and recreate itself, and to transform uniquely wherever the community dispersed. From Merengue and Santeria of Cuba, to Capoeira and Feijoada of Brazil, to the Blues, Jazz, and so-called "soul food" of the United States, no matter what expression manifested into culture, beliefs, diet, or politics, the African roots of the tree for me are the prefix—literally, what comes before—all other subsequent qualities. Therefore, rather than African, I use Afro- to represent the full complexity of all that can be called "African" in the new world.

This is how I define myself about the "African Experience." The book will be written from the unique perspective of the so-called African diaspora, but more importantly from the unique viewpoint of a person who sincerely sees the world from a global view. My reasons for going to Africa were threefold. I was looking for adventure, opportunity, and most importantly the chance to make a change in a place that I felt so connected to. I truly believe that travel liberates a person and allows them to reinvent themselves, while in the process enabling them to discover new approaches to life's challenges.

My experiences traveling to Africa would also show me that leaving one's home is humbling and disorienting. After my travels, blackness became something I just didn't take for granted; it became an actual defining characteristic for me back in the United States. It also became clearer that historically, we Americans of different races have defined ourselves in opposition to one another. Africa is of course much larger and much more heterogeneous than my limited personal journey can ever convey. In the end, Africa would help me to find a lost part of myself, gain a wider sense of purpose, and to reconnect with humanity on a multi-dimensional level that transcends social, racial, political, or economic barriers.

To my parents, Ada & Myers Evans: You gave me vision to see.

To my sister, Marla-Tiye Vieira, Thanks for inspiring me.

To Sarah: A beautiful spirit, friend, and fellow seeker

Contents

Chapter One

Africa Was Born In Me

*"What is Africa to me, Copper Sun or Scarlet Sea, Jungle Track, Strong
Bronzed Men, or Regal Black Women from whose Loins I sprang when the
Birds of Eden sang? One three Centuries removed from the Scene his Fathers
loved, Spicy Grove, Cinnamon Tree, what is Africa to me?"*
—*Countee Cullen*

My first African adventure began in earnest in early June 2002,
but in reality, the psychological journey began on my birthday,
June 21, 1971. As a small child growing up in the suburbs of
Atlantic City, New Jersey, I was always acutely aware of my blackness. I saw
it sometimes as an obstacle to be overcome, and other times viewed it as a
badge of uniqueness and honor in a sea of overwhelming whiteness. There
was always the distinct mark of being different in the primarily Caucasian
school district. I can recall as far back as the third grade dreading the
month of February because of its identification as "Black History Month."
Looking at pictures of Harriet Tubman, Fredrick Douglass, and other great
black leaders would leave me with the ironic sense of both embarrassment
and pride, as the vast majority of my white classmates chuckled under
their breaths reflecting an odd mixture of condescension and fear. This

same source of embarrassment would motivate me later to seek out an African-centered worldview.

As a young child, I remember identifying with television series such as *The Love Boat*, *S.W.A.T.*, *The Bionic Man*, and big screen icons such as James Bond and the Pink Panther. Childhood innocence is truly a wonderful thing. It allows you to experience all the joys, dreams, and hopes of life, keeping one grounded in the ultimate sense of possibilities. My identification with these fictional characters was based on their sense of adventure, their ability to overcome great odds and their deep sense of justice. I don't think that my admiration was very different from most American youth my age. Growing up, I had the fortune or rather misfortune of having a father who was a police detective. I can remember looking back and thinking that his job was the ultimate symbol of all that was brave, strong, and right in the world. I remember thinking at the time that my father was the most powerful man on earth and that he represented the safety and justice of the state. |Paradoxically, as I matured and grew, these very symbols would come to account for the oppression of my ancestors, my people, and more directly, myself. In later years, I began to see myself in contention to the very things I used to hold in such high esteem. In time, the very things that allowed me to make sense of my world began to feel like a large dark gray wall blocking me from a sense of self-expression and freedom.

As I matured, I came to understand the larger social dynamics within the country; it became apparent that the very people who were socially, politically, and economically marginalized were also the ones whom the state and law enforcement seemed to attack. This was a disturbing revelation, to say the least, and encouraged me to seek an alternative perspective and separate reality. I was trying to complete those vague memories, nebulous pictures of the past and present, and missing meanings, as I found myself growing up and unclear about the very social and cultural fabric in which I was raised. It is sometimes tough for other Americans to truly empathize with the deep disconnect that majority of Afro-Americans feel, consciously or unconsciously, growing up within their own country. We often wear our ancestral mask, born in the land of milk and honey, an environment, which yields no true self-reflection, but only allows one to see and thus measure our worth through the eyes of others. This duality sings its song in our aesthetics, our education, sports, religion, and most tellingly in the national media.

At the age of eighteen, I graduated from high school and joined the Navy. It was a form of escape and a cure from the wanderlust that was ever cultivating in my psyche, which was expanding and yearning to discover itself and which would forever encapsulate my being for years to come. Looking through a hazy window after a fresh rainstorm abandoned its outpouring, the question continued to loom heavy that there had to be another world out there, a place that would be able to see me for all that I was, an environment that would not try to narrow my concepts or dampen my inner fire. Ironically, both my internal and external global journey would begin in a very unlikely place; Tijuana, Mexico.

Mexico was my first voyage abroad. This adventure laid the foundation for me to feel an immense sense of freedom and possibility living abroad. For the first time in my life, I felt as if people were looking at me as a person, not just a color. Traveling through the seedy streets of the Mexican border town with my fellow Naval buddies, most of us young and naive, we were oblivious to the latent dangers that caroused the city. In retrospect,

Tijuana was an undeveloped border town with an enormous amount of poverty and crime. Most locals perceived us as potential meal tickets, an extension of American wealth and power, or at least the image of that material gluttony. What I didn't realize was that my being an American far outweighed my blackness; one stereotype eclipsed the other. At that time, little did I realize that this would be a forewarning of things to come much later during my travels in Africa. At this juncture in my life, freedom seemed like freedom. This would further harden my perception that the racial/color problem was bred, fueled, and maintained in the social reality that was America. In the midst of my great revelation, I was blind to the hundreds of disenfranchised native Indians who were homeless and disempowered staring me right in the face. It's funny how human beings can be so narrowed by their own biases, experiences, and outlooks that they often easily overlook or rationalize profound examples of injustices because they aren't somehow connected to their own immediate reality. Nevertheless, my first experience out of the country really left me with a positive sense of longing for what was beyond the borders of the US culturally, socially, politically, and spiritually.

My next step toward merging with the theory of social transformation, specifically Pan-African ideas came during my time as a student at Temple University in Philadelphia. Temple is one of the better schools for African American studies, and is located directly in the heart of North Philadelphia, which in the early '90s was a mecca of Afro-centric thought and awareness. At that time, there was a fresh vibrancy connecting with old philosophical ideals of Negritude. The result was a rebirth of what we call Afro-centricity, literally Afro-centeredness. For a young African American male like me, this seemed like a new revolutionary paradigm; a way of looking at the world that set reality upside down, as though a great storm had come and blown winds of much-needed life back into the empty promises of stale history books, which had plagued and haunted me from childhood. The essence of the theory is that those belonging to the African diaspora need to have African culture, thought patterns, and learning concepts centered in their everyday reality. In actuality, this intellectual movement started much earlier with writers such as Aimé Césaire and a movement called Negritude. He was a revolutionary intellectual thinker and poet from the French Caribbean island of Martinique. Césaire, along with other black intellectuals of his day, started a movement, which stated that African culture, history, and spirituality, could only be understood by African thought processes and by placing Africa at the epicenter of its descendants' worldview.

This seemed like the answer that I had been seeking, a solution to my social problems or at least a formulation of the questions that needed to be reconciled. I read everything that I could get my hands on concerning the history of ancient African cultures, black cultural symbolism, and the vast intricacies of hidden traditional African religions. Afro-centric thought stressed that we should consider ourselves part of the larger African diaspora, and reinforced within us the understanding that our political, social, and economic situations are connected with the historical and social stream of African realities. I became immersed in this thought system and felt that I needed to experience a more tangible expression of this reality. Temple University provided the perfect opportunity to engage and explore my fervid desires.

That first semester, I joined an organization aptly named Afro-Centricity United, which provided the perfect environment to integrate my emerging black consciousness with real-world activism and work. The founder was Joseph Coquitos, an Afro-Puerto Rican Santeria practitioner from Harlem, New York. I would later find out that his family was part of an African indigenous religion sometimes named Santeria, Candomblé, and Voodoo, with centers reaching throughout the West Indies and North, Central, and South America. This ancient religion has its origins with the Yoruba and Ewe people of southwestern Nigeria and Benin. These ancient belief systems were brought to America during the slave trade and were adaptable enough to maintain their cultural roots for over a hundred years. For me, this discovery was akin to learning that I was part of a living relic of Africa that transcended time, space, and location. It was like taking a spiritual time ship into a cultural buffet of ancient delights and vast memories of days gone by with whispers from people from long ago. Speaking with Joe Coquitos about this new religion was familiar as it was foreign. He told fascinating stories about black Gods such as Ogun, the god of War, and Shango, the god of Fire. After conducting research, I also learned that Haitian Voodoo was a derivative of this same West African system. An elaborate and often berated complex religious-philosophical system, Voodoo has often been demonized in the Western media. I learned of brave rebels fighting against great odds and the black genius generals of the Haitian revolution who were inspired by sacrifices to these same African Gods. These people, heroes of Voodoo, led to the western hemisphere's first independent black nation.

This intense spiritual and cultural search led me to visit a Santeria temple in New York City. All the books in the world could not accurately define the exuberant, intense, and vibrant feeling of an experiential fellowship within a Yoruba celebration. There were drummers from all over the African Diaspora; Trinidad, Puerto Rico, Cuba, Harlem, Los Angeles, and West Africa. As we approached the apartment building, a lovely duplex located in the heart of Brooklyn's upscale park slope neighborhood, the erratic and moving sounds of drumming intensified, and the smell of incense infused the air. The hallway was in stark contrast to the quiet and uniformed area outside. There were African masks, richly painted symbols, tropical plants, and exotic ritual costumes. As we sat down, there seemed to be a drumming showdown between an Afro-American drummer and a musician from Senegal. The drummer from Senegal had condescendingly called him a Yankee! Well, this created musical fireworks and started what is known as a face off in many circles of traditional African communities. It became a very vigorous musical event with both players beating rhythmic tunes, alternating back and forth, pushing one another to the edge of exhaustion and creative intensity. This competition surely made the entire room feel as if we had stepped into a remote Nigerian village where time was suspended, and spirit was as tangible as the clothes on our backs. After an hour of playing, the drummer from New York, William Bell, was declared the winner. William was very well known in Santeria circles as a *Brujo*, which means witch or sorcerer. I was told that he was also a priest of Palo, a very different type of African religion which was brought over by Central African slaves and has been preserved in such places as Brazil, Surinam, Cuba, and Puerto Rico. Many considered Palo to be the most direct method of communication with ancestral spirits. Its beliefs are strongly animistic and have direct bearing with other forms of shamanistic understandings of the world. All that exists is considered to be inhabited by a conscious or energetic life force. Man is placed in a unique juncture that represents a doorway into this unknown realm, and through the gift of mediumship, we can pierce this veil.

The spirits that are most relevant in Palo are the spirits of the dead, also known as the *egun*. It's because of this close relationship with death and the dead that Palo has been layered with such negative speculation, as well as fear. Unlike the West African systems, which place emphasis on the forces of nature such as the Goddess of the Sea Yemaya, the God of Iron and War Ogun, and the Goddess of lakes and fresh water Osun, Palo's essential practices include necromancy, which involves communicating through death and magic. Necromancy, and specifically as used in Palo, has its primary worship and practice in a consecrated cauldron. This cauldron is often suffused with sacred plants, herbs, earth, and many times with "human bones." This magical pot is believed to be inhabited by the spirit of the dead, which in turn acts as an interface for all religious ceremonies within the system. To be initiated into the Palo religion, it's necessary to undergo a ceremony called Rayamiento; the act of cutting. This ceremony involves an experienced priest placing special marks on the skin of the new initiate. A sacred pact is thus made between the spirit that lives in the cauldron and the person. This practice is still alive and well in most Central African communities today, and can be traced directly back to its original ancestral sources.

William Bell was an imposing figure, standing six feet tall with penetrating auburn-colored eyes, an intense stare, and an inner confidence that boarded on swagger. He had a reputation for being quite a ladies' man, as well as being an excellent diviner or reader. He finally approached me and asked, "are you a new member of this Santeria house?" I responded, "I am a guest of Joseph Coquitos." He was very persuasive with words and possessed a dark charm which immediately drew me into his orbit. William shared the hidden dimensions of these religions and how they were birthed in Africa, nurtured in Afro-Latin American culture, and eventually expressed in the Black-American communities here in North America. I asked him the context of his use of the word matured.

He stated, "Black-American musician Chris Olayano was the First Afro-American of non-Latin extraction to be initiated into Santeria." William began showcasing his remarkable skills as a storyteller by fusing politics and culture into the history of these black spiritual systems. He eloquently articulated the heroic deeds of a famous female rebel leader in Haiti whose ritualistic sacrificing of a black pig marked the beginning of that county's Revolution for Independence. He spoke of the famous Maroon colonies of black rebels in the Caribbean, and of the homegrown hoodoo communities in the South America.

"Traditional African religious systems in the new world can be the bridge that fills the gap between our lost ancestral roots, thus fueling an incubus, cultural, and spiritual rebirth."

Even during these young and idealistic times, I was somewhat skeptical of such grandiose claims.

Time seemed to have stopped at this point with one grand scheme often melting into another. To my surprise, Joseph began to perform a ritualistic dance. This particular dance was dedicated to the African god Aganyu, representative of the energy of the desert, the wilderness, and the mighty volcano. This particular African god was synchronized with the Catholic Saint Christopher, patron of travelers. The drumming became extremely intense. His movements were precise, measured, passionate, paradoxically frantic, and controlled simultaneously. During these forceful dances, the Santeria community claimed that the person was being possessed by his/her guardian spirit. I personally thought that the dancer was just responding to cultural and social learned behaviors and communal rituals at the time. However, one could never be completely sure unless one was a direct participant in the act itself. I was left with a sense of wonder and extreme curiosity. I can remember returning to Philadelphia with a new sense of pride and mission. I wanted to be a cultural custodian, a preserver of the mythical, ancient, and noble African continuum that had been brutally taken away from my ancestors. I immediately contacted my friend and told him about my newfound discovery. I shared with him how this new deeper understanding of African religion could enhance our ideas about social building, and how this new connectedness would allow us to build schools and institutions perhaps in the inner cities. He was as excited as I was, although he added his own element of discourse, which was just part of his competitive makeup.

In the following months, I spoke with as many folks involved with the Santeria community as possible. We journeyed back to New York City to get our heads marked and find out which force of nature, *orisa*, would guide us. In order to find this out, we would have to get a spiritual reading by a *Babalawo*, considered the equivalent of the Pope in the Catholic religion. We searched for the address in the eclectic neighborhood of Brooklyn's Park Slope. I had the concurrent feelings of anxiety, excitement, and fear. We rang the doorbell twice before a very attractive honey-colored woman in her early 40s answered the door. She greeted us and led us into the apartment which was more spacious than it had appeared from the outside. She took our coats and brought us a very strong-tasting tea, which she described as a special recipe which came from Cuba. Her name was

Galoni, and she was the wife of Otunji, the high priest that we'd come to see.

After waiting for more than ten minutes, which seemed like a lifetime, he entered the room slowly with a confident deliberation that reflected a deep-seated belief in his abilities and status. He wasn't very imposing, as might be expected for someone of his religious standing. However, his power became clearly evident by his depth of knowledge and mental profundity. He spoke with a very insightful and lucid tone. He had a sharp eye for the finer subtle nuances, which as I would find out much later, are so intricate to understanding black culture, or any cultural expression for that matter. Otunji told us that he was a fifth generation Babalawo, West African high priest, who had been raised on a small farm twenty miles south of Lagos, Nigeria. He said, "this indigenous Nigerian religion was a part of my family for hundreds of years before the days of British colonialism."

Considered the high priest of the Santeria religion, his position is mainly judicial, and followers in extremely difficult and ambiguous situations consulted him. He is considered the only one that can determine who is the ruling orisa of an individual. The ceremony is widely known as *bajar an Orunla*, the bringing down of Orunla. He is the patron saint of the Babalawo and energy of divination. He is syncretized with the Catholic saint St. Francis of Assisi.

According to the West African Yoruba tradition, this specific orisa is considered the energy or path of divination which was present during God's creation on earth. Therefore, his priests are considered the foremost authority on the secret destiny of each human being, and it's only through this process that many practitioners believe that one can ever realize the sacred covenant that each of us had consolidated during our birth. Reincarnation then becomes an essential part of indigenous African spiritual philosophy, as each individual comes to earth with a particular destiny to fulfill, an individual way of reaching our highest good and expanding our universal consciousness. A very symbolically enriching story surrounding this orisa tells how Orunmila was able to trick Death (Iku) into prolonging any individual's life by wearing his sacred colors, alternating green and yellow, in a bracelet or *ide*. Because of his supposed pact with Death, this orisa also knows the time that a person's life will expire.

What intrigues me about this system is its elaborate, ancient, and sophisticated divination system. This is considered the very foundation and crux of the religion. The Babalawo uses three divination systems; the Opele, the Opon Ifa, and the Ikin. The opele (pronounced okuele) consists of an iron chain that connects eight oval medallions created with coconut rinds, although they can also be made with ivory, bone, copper, or silver. Each medallion has a different design on each of its two sides. The high priest throws down the opele, and he holds the chain by the middle, ensuring that the medallions fall four on each side, parallel to each other. Sixteen different designs can be made by the opele. Each pattern is known as an oddu. The combination of sixteen oddus forms 256 new designs, each of which is accompanied by a verse and by one or more *patakis*, or stories. The Babalawo translates the person's fate according to the verse and the pataki. Each oddu is accompanied by a specific orisa as well as a set of prayers known as *suyeres*.

This divination system comprises all of the knowledge of the universe and the entire past, present, and future. The more learned and talented a

Babalawo, the more folk stories he will be able to recite. The more stories he can remember, the more accurate his readings, and the higher his standing within the community. My friend and I seemed to have lucked out, as this high priest was world-renowned and had an impeccable reputation.

Speaking with a very disarming and laid-back manner which made both Laguane and myself very comfortable and relaxed, he suddenly announced that he was ready to divine and asked who would like to go first, with a half-knowing smile. My friend was quick to raise his hand and in his usual headfirst, do or die demeanor, went off into the back room with the Babalawo to find out what we'd been speculating about for so long. Who are our guarding African angels, orisas? After about forty minutes, my friend and the priest returned, with Laguane looking gravely disappointed. With anxious anticipation, I asked him which African God spoke. He very humbly stated OSHUN! Well, this came as a great surprise to both of us. First of all, being typical macho young men, we exclusively focused on the male deities. The Babalawo explained, "There is nothing demeaning about having a female guardian orisa, especially Oshun. She is the guardian of love, arts, and relationships. The majority of her children seemed to be infused by their relationships with the opposite sex and interpersonal dynamics in general."

This last point really hit true with my friend, who since I could remember had always been tremendously influenced by his romantic interest. This spiritual path was like a river, a reflection, through which one might know himself or herself through a partner, living and expressing creatively within one's heart. Oshun was the African Venus personified.

As time passed, I became open to anything; outwardly eager, enthusiastic, and slightly expectant. Inside, there was deep conflict over

13

what would seem to be this moment of truth. I felt nervous and unsure, hesitant of the unknown, unclear about what I would do if I found what I was actually looking for. The quest for this vague truth at that moment didn't seem as pressing. We entered a small room that was filled with strange-looking African figurines and bottles filled with unknown substances. The smell of burnt wood and incense permeated the air.

Otunji explained that each figurine was a representative of a particular orisha or African god, and he took out a wooden tray with intricately designed beautiful ethnic patterns. This was the famous tray of *Ifa*, the fabled mouth of the gods, the highest and most accurate divination voice in the Santeria religion.

He took a deep gasp as he kissed his divining chain before beginning the prayer in his native Nigerian tongue. The prayer was somewhat disorienting; the words were foreign, alien, but somehow familiar and comforting.

After ten minutes of prayers and calling out to his ancestral lineage, he gently tossed the chain four times in a vertical direction, up and down, down and up, stating, "Each pattern is the interpretation of a specific *oddu*, story."

He then grabbed a piece of white chalk and gently marked my head after saying a specific prayer again. He then proceeded to tell me that my guardian orisa was OYA! This was even more of a surprise; in African Mythology, Oya is the powerful female warrior that represents the wind, death, transformation, and every aspect of change. The priest says, "your journey will be filled with spiritual profundity, deep transformations, and exploration of foreign cultures and lands. Struggle will characterize your life's work against injustice, challenging the status quo, and being a catalyst for change, both for others and yourself. You walk very close to your ancestors (the dead), those in your family lineage that have passed on to the other side."

Seeing the world with youthful naïveté, I had once again overlooked the wider realities of what was being told to me and the profound implications that they would play in my future. I can remember being more disappointed at not having a male guardian African God, as opposed to truly contemplating the future challenges that came up in this reading. At the end of our reading, we were each charged $200, which for two unemployed, part-time college students was an exuberant amount! To add insult to injury, the Babalawo stated, "each of you must pay $6000 to be fully initiated into this priesthood." This would be the first of many experiences in dealing with wily, callous, and often ravenous opportunists that can be so deeply systemic within the cultural fabric of Africanism, especially cannibalistic in their deceptive ability to exploit people that are sincerely trying to reconnect with their ancestral roots.

This struck a disappointing cord with us both. Driving back to Philadelphia very little was verbalized. However, there was a shared unspoken covenant in the realization of the complexity and dangers that lay ahead upon this unparalleled journey to find wholeness in a living cultural river that now seemed as distant as the moon. Between the two of us, there was an unspoken realization of the complexity of seeking completeness in a culture in which we felt was so apart from our very beings.

Even after this very disappointing experience, I was still compelled to immerse myself in the works of writers such as Frantz Fanon, Molefi Asante, Dr. Henry Clark, Ayikway Armah, and Cheikh Anta Diop. These were some of the looming pioneer giants in the world of intellectual

Africanism. Future experiences would indeed reveal that no amount of intellectualization could ever suffice for actual experiential contact in helping one to come to terms with the deep complexities which are the whole mark of the African culture and historical dynamic which I so desperately sought.

During my senior year, I landed an internship with the ANC, The African National Congress. This was the most widely known and admired of the African liberation groups, which was founded by the charismatic and devoted Nelson Mandela. There was such magic in the air, a fire of optimism, and the hope of a new tomorrow at that time. Nelson Mandela was finally released, Apartheid had ended, and there was the talk of South Africa becoming a multi-racial democracy. Well, it seemed as if I had died and gone to heaven. I was a college student able to mix and mingle with some of the world's greatest freedom liberators and thinkers from Africa. My first day was very surprising. I was bemused by what I perceived to be a lack of professionalism that pervaded the ANC's office. Most of the staff was receptive towards me because I was American as opposed to being a black. Instead of asking me questions about the struggle that Afro-Americans faced during our own apartheid/civil rights struggle, they seemed to be more concerned and interested in popular American culture. I was asked several times about celebrities and famous entertainers such as Tupac Shakur, athletes such as Michael Jordan, and actresses like Whitney Houston. I was totally taken aback by this superficial way of relating, particularly by the black South Africans belonging to the ANC. How fate can sometimes throw us curveballs. The one member who seemed to be the most interested in the political and social views of Afro-Americans was a white South African of British descent.

Her name was Lisa Braxton, and she was a volunteer with the African National Congress office in Washington D.C. Soft-spoken with sad yet expressive blue eyes, she was cordial, yet distant and aloof. Seemingly, in two places at once. I can remember speaking with her and feeling as if she was looking for something vague and inexplicable; it was as if she were trying to penetrate beyond the surface veneer of what was being stated with the veil of words into something more tangible. Her questions about the political struggles here in the United States were poignant and sincere. Nevertheless, there was a haunting questioning in her eyes that gave me the sense of someone who was concealing a tremendous sense of guilt and maybe even shame. Maybe this feeling of remorse steamed from her thoughts of how I perceived her people within the context of Apartheid. In retrospect, perhaps she was just mirroring my energy back, which may have been unconsciously closed and somewhat guarded. Despite this, the meeting was forthcoming and rather enlightening on many subjects. She explained, "my family is of Afrikaans descent and I was raised in a small town north-west of Durban, (a large city located in the south eastern portion of South Africa). My family was always supportive of liberal politics and totally sympathetic of the ANC's vision."

This incredulous meeting would be a prelude of things to come in the future. "Africa defies Western logic, is often contradictory, and yet shows us universal truths."

I left this meeting feeling a little confused yet knowing that there was a life-altering lesson to be learned from this diminutive lady. It would be years before these omens would speak in a cohesive message, the deeper layers of which I would eventually comprehend.

After giving three months of dedicated volunteer service to the ANC, I was disappointed to find out that other foreign volunteers along with myself, would not be able to meet with Nelson Mandela, as we had been assured at the beginning. We were initially told that we interns had a high chance of meeting both Nelson Mandela and ex-President Botha. Obviously, the majority of us were much more interested in meeting with Mr. Mandela. There were, however, a few, just for the historical significance on such a monumental level, who would have been happy to meet with anyone even slightly connected with this event. The fact that we weren't able to be a part of this great historical happening would have been okay if it had been a simple issue of logistics. Upon closer examination, we discovered that there was never any intention on the part of the ANC to allow the non-South African interns to ever meet Mr. Mandela. I found this type of deceit and blatant callousness to be appalling. These challenges occur in every organization and every culture. However, this underhanded non-accountability is far too pervasive in too many African institutions. One has only to look at the economic, social, and political woes and challenges to ascertain this destructive dynamic in full force. Even with my complex and vast experiences with Africanism here in the US, there is nothing that can prepare a person that has been culturally acclimated in the west for the large cultural rift that is confronted with living and working on the continent itself.

In June of 2002, my African adventure would move from the mere realm of intellectual speculation into the full blossoming of experiential reality, and with that, my transmutation and growth truly began.

Chapter Two

Echoes of Kilimanjaro

"Africa is a fever in the blood."
—Doris Lessing

My first trip to Africa was in June 2002. I flew to the East African country of Tanzania, a land steeped in cultural mythology and the historical embodiment of the pan-African doctrine. Much of Tanzania's mythos and doctrine is based on the philosophy of the late Julius Nyerere, a scholar-leader who led the country out of the colonial yoke of British domination into the high principles of socialism, *uhuru,* which is Kiswahili for freedom. It was in Tanzania that President Nyerere summarized the collective vision of the continent with his progress forward into the 21st Century. He believed that only indigenous cultural values would solve African problems. He declared Kiswahili as the national language. It was as a result of this that even Shakespeare's works were translated into Kiswahili; a first for an African language. Tanzania was one of the few countries on the continent that actually utilized an indigenous language for all official business.

During the formative years of independence, a flame was lit on the top of Mount Kilimanjaro symbolizing the freedom, dignity, and majestic spirit of African people. This symbolic representation was meant to inspire

not just Tanzanians, but the entire continent of Africa. Many people
have asked if Nyerere's grand plan of collective responsibility was simply
an idealist's dream that cost his country millions of dollars in foreign
investment dollars. During the early years of Nyerere's presidency, the
infrastructure in Tanzania was one of the worst on the continent if not the
world. There was very little local industry of any significance throughout
the country. Nevertheless, to me, Tanzania was a cultural mecca unlike
anywhere else in Africa. It was a moral guiding light in the midst of what
looked to be decaying and decadent neo-colonized countries pretending
at independence. What Tanzania lacked in material progress, it more than
made up for with its high ethics and principles-first foreign policy. I was
in deep admiration of its most monumental achievement; the ability to
synthesize the catastrophic effects of tribalism. This social cancer has beset
most of Tanzania's neighbors in Eastern Africa—Rwanda being the place
where tribalism reached its height of depravity. A primary rationale for the
lack of tribal warfare and ethnic politics in Tanzania has been the unifying
effects of its national language, Swahili.

My perception of Tanzania was that of a country with a mission of
a saint, synchronized in many ways with Dostoevsky's character Prince
Myshkin in *The Idiot*. Coming of age during The Cold War, Tanzania
was seduced and pulled by two mistresses, much in the same way that
Prince Myshkin's character was. In the case of Tanzania, these divergent
powers were capitalism and socialism. Like the prince, it seemed that the
more charity and generosity the country showed to the world, the more
condemnation the West aimed at it. Whether it was indigenous social
economic reforms or principled foreign policies, each step seemed to have
bought about international isolation and economic stagnation. Consider

Tanzania's invasion of its neighbor Uganda, which was undertaken without any outside support, to rid the region of one of the world's worst dictators, Idi Amin. Once again, a noble act brought about disastrous consequences. This strategy almost led the country into bankruptcy. Tanzania was also one of the first countries to cut off diplomatic and economic relations with South Africa, which is the political powerhouse of the region. Once again Tanzania demonstrated its willingness to make decisions based on principles as opposed to practical self-interest.

Arriving in the country, my first day was like a blur. The flight from New York's Kennedy Airport to Dar El Salaam took eighteen hours. When I arrived at the airport in the capital, I had to wait at least an hour before I was able to collect my luggage. Sitting at the airport bar lounge, the overwhelming scope of my journey finally hit me! I truly realized that I was halfway around the world in a country that I had never been to, meeting a person or rather a family whom I knew virtually nothing about, and to make matters worse, I had a severe case of air sickness. This consisted of dizziness, stomach cramps, and vomiting. I also suffered from jet lag, which luckily hadn't fully set in. My anxiety began to grow as I noticed a large group of people standing outside the window holding name signs as a way for the passengers to recognize their respective family, friends, and associates as they came off the plane. As I looked closer, I noticed my name, misspelled but nevertheless, still my name, being put up by a stout dark man with very friendly eyes and an inviting smile. As I waved my hand up to get his attention, he seemed to have already recognized me. His eyes looked at me very openly and with a curious twinkle, almost as if he were meeting a long lost relative. I approached and asked if he was Mr. Musuma. He quietly confirmed with a nod and a shy smile. I nervously sat there awaiting my luggage which was arriving from Kennedy Airport in New York. As I waited, I thought to myself what I would do if nothing arrived, if my luggage went to the wrong destination. Thousands of miles away from home, what could I do? Luckily, nothing was lost, and all my luggage arrived in a very timely and organized manner. In retrospect, everything seemed surreal. I was finally in the land of my ancestors, the land of so much mythology, the land of my distant hopes, wishes, and dreams, yet I felt as if someone needed to wake me from a dream, to remind me that I was no longer fantasizing about this supposed African utopia, but it was now experiential.

I gathered my luggage and headed out of the airport. The first thing I observed was that Tanzanian women would avoid direct eye contact at any cost! My first reaction was to take it personally. I wondered if there was something wrong with me, maybe it was what I was wearing, or maybe it was the fact that I had a shaved head. Different types of ideas seemed to come into my head when I was over 5,000 miles away from home and had jetlag. As I drove back through the African night, we naturally began to engage in conversation about our previous travels. He went on to tell me about his myriad of experiences traveling overseas as a consultant for a European telecommunications company that was based in Tanzania.

To my surprise, Mr. Musoma was extremely well traveled, beginning from his college days in Great Britain, where he attained an MBA, up until more recently his multiple trips to the Middle East and Asia. He also spoke of his children's experiences in the United States. He told me that despite having wonderful times abroad, he wouldn't choose to live anywhere except Tanzania. I found this to be very strange. I guess I was coming from the opposite perspective about feeling at home in our respective countries. I have always had wanderlust regarding places outside of my home in the USA. However, my passion for traveling has always been tainted with the perspective of finding a place that feels like home, a place with a sense of belonging, a place where I would be judged by the content of my character and not the color of my skin. Here I was in the land of my dreams, Mother Africa—the mistress of my lost ancestors, the womb of creation, and the progenies of mankind.

We finally arrived at Mr. Musoma's home around 9 p.m. after what seemed like endless driving in part due to my disorientation at my new surroundings as well as my jetlag. A 5'3" woman, the first lady of the home, who introduced herself as Mr. Musoma's wife, immediately greeted me. She looked much younger than him and had a cute, girlish, almost innocent look to her. He introduced the next two ladies as his daughters. The older of the two was named Shona. She had very dark, smooth skin along with piercing sad black eyes, giving her a strange wisdom beyond her years. The younger daughter's name was Nafia, and she had caramel-colored skin, an almost copper hue, with very short brown hair and a warm smile. The eldest daughter reminded me of the women at the airport; guarded, shy, withdrawn, and somewhat aloof. As she greeted me, her eyes immediately dropped to the floor. In the west, this would be an indication that the person was hiding something, didn't have good intentions, or was simply lacking confidence. As I would later find out, this is certainly not the case in Tanzania or throughout East Africa in general.

In Tanzania, it's always polite to give some type of gift when visiting someone's home for the first time. After all of the formalities and gift exchanges had concluded, I was shown to my bedroom. It was a relatively small room with one single bed, with pictures of different outdated

American musicians, such as Madonna, Prince, and Michael Jackson. After unpacking my things, I went into the washroom and began to brush my teeth. It was then that I realized there wasn't any running water in the house! My heart dropped. What was I going to do? How was I going to go to the bathroom, shave, take a hot bath, etc.? My heart almost jumped out from my chest. As I walked into the other room, Nafia entered. "There isn't any plumbing in the house because it is still being built," she said. However, she assured me not to worry since they gathered all their water from a local well outside. Shortly afterward, the eldest daughter came by the door and left two huge pots, one with warm water and the other with cool water. One pot was for bathing, and the other was for brushing and rinsing off the teeth.

Shortly afterward I thought to myself, *Now I can finally retire into my bedroom and get some type of privacy and sleep!* The bed was hard and slightly uncomfortable, however, after spending over eighteen hours on crowded airplanes and in empty despotic airports, this seemed really welcoming. No sooner did I lay down and started to doze off, when I suddenly noticed that someone came into the room and lay at the other end of the bed. He stared at me for a minute and then introduced himself as Andre. He said that we would be sharing this room and that he was euphoric to meet someone from America. I just sat there thinking that this was turning into a living nightmare; no water and sharing my bed with some strange man. It was reminiscent of my first night at boot camp years ago! Needless to say, I didn't get very much sleep that evening. Here I was miles away from everything familiar, safe, or even logical, and as far as I could see, it felt like a nightmare. I lay throughout the night, too tired to sleep, yet too sleepy to think straight. Pondering on the real reasons that I was here in Africa, I asked myself what I was seeking. What was I running from? Would I find what I was looking for in a place that seemed familiar from afar, but which up close seemed strange and alien?

Halfway through the night, I was able to doze off for three hours, before being awakened by the sounds of coo-cooing roosters. I realized that this would be my natural alarm clock for the remainder of my time in Tanzania. I got up and went into the washroom. Two full, large buckets awaited me. One was filled with cool water and the other with warm water. All the ladies of the house were up and preparing breakfast, doing the washing, and cleaning up. As I would find out, in most traditional Sub-Saharan African societies, this is the norm. As convenient as this was for me, it seemed unfair to watch the men sit back and do absolutely nothing around the house while the women broke their backs with labor.

During this time, I would have described myself as an Afro-centric Universalist, however, I was unconsciously reflecting a deep American value system. I noticed it not just in my judgment of the inequality of the sex roles which I immediately perceived, but also in the general lack of amenities and infrastructure which I observed in the home where I was staying. In the morning, Mr. Musoma and I headed downtown to the city center of Dar Es Salaam. We took a very old white Pajaro Jeep, which he took the most pride in. Driving down the dirt roads of Dar Es Salaam, I could see why he was so proud of his jeep. Unlike in the USA where large 4x4 vehicles are a status symbol, in many African nations, they are a necessity. To describe the level of underdevelopment of most of the roads in Tanzania would leave most Westerners appalled. My trip would later reveal on a much deeper level that African culture is nothing if not resilient and adaptable. As we continued to travel closer to downtown

Dar Es Salaam, the physical typography reminded me of a small southern town in rural Georgia, with its small, charming but somewhat dilapidated shanty homes dotting the sides of the red dirt roads. As we approached Mr. Musoma's place of work, I was further reminded of the Deep South with the hospitality and simple ease of pace in which many of the people moved.

He worked at a large telecommunications company owned by a group of Dutch investors. The building was in the heart of downtown next to the exclusive Holiday Inn and other upscale structures. When I entered the building, I was amazed that all of the entry-level workers were native Tanzanians, while all of the upper-level management were of European ancestry. I was immediately appalled by this dynamic. I was thousands of miles away from home, and I was looking at the same form of discrimination that had made me leave my home country. Shortly after being introduced to everyone in the office, we left to eat traditional Tanzanian cuisine. This traditional cuisine consisted of large chunks of beef called *yama-choma* and a corn-based food called *ugali* that was similar to grits. This was the most popular and widespread indigenous cuisine throughout East Africa, specifically Tanzania, Uganda, and Kenya. Later that day, we went back to Mr. Musoma's home, where I quickly found the time to get a couple of hours of sleep before being awakened by the sounds of voices outside my window. I looked out of my window and suddenly saw half of the neighborhood outside. To my surprise, Mr. Musoma also owned a small neighborhood store, and it was a gathering point for everyone in the area during the weekend. There was a faint knock on my door, and I could hear Nafia's soft voice saying that everyone wanted me to join them outside. I told her surely, and quickly gathered my jeans, put on a shirt, and hurried outside. When I went outside, I was greeted with the words *habari gani*, which is a Kiswahili greeting with a similar meaning as hello. However, I noticed that some of the younger folks would greet with the words, *sheek o moo*. I found this to be a little confusing as I didn't recognize this phrase from any of my Kiswahili books. As I would later find out, this greeting is reserved by younger Tanzanians towards those they consider an elder or at least out of their age group; it's a sign of respect.

I thought it amazing to have a different verbal expression as a way of showing deference for someone with more life experience. Culturally, this was in sharp contrast to the USA, where there is a tendency to disregard our elderly and dread the entire aging process. It is a matter of conceptualization. In many parts of Africa, time is seen as flexible, interconnected, and cyclical, whereas in the West, especially the United States, time is conceived as linear, and old age is something to be overcome and stopped—an inevitable disappointment in life to be avoided for as long as possible. I would soon find out that each of these conceptions has both advantages and disadvantages. The concept of time in Tanzania reached beyond just themes of intergenerational relationships. I would discover in practical terms that time agreements hold different meaning here than in the west. The concept of time in Tanzania isn't rigidly defined as it is in the west. Although this allows for less stress and sometimes more meaningful relationships between people, it also creates a high level of inefficiency and lack of professionalism that seems to permeate a myriad of social and cultural dynamics. Again, I was looking through a value system that is based on my own cultural upbringing, and experiencing an entirely different perspective of life that creates a sense of disorientation, which forces one to anchor onto what is familiar, known, and trusted. I would later recognize how to transform my cognitive understanding to truly assimilate and immerse myself in an entirely foreign value dynamic. Visiting a country and indeed merging with it, bonding with it beyond just reflecting and voicing the local norms are two totally separate approaches. To touch a culture from the surface only is to observe and then judge its people, places, and history from one's own experience. Many times this happens on an unconscious level, as we project what is important in our own cultural mirror onto another. Judging how things should be done, how people should relate, and what they should prioritize based on our own value systems is a limited approach to interacting with others. To truly connect oneself with a culture is to experience the other with an open mind, to look through the kaleidoscope of reality that is often nebulous in the beginning. Only after confrontation can one honestly say what an authentic experience is. When I speak of language, I am talking more about the subtle flow of exchange between people in a culture, the dynamism of how people inter-relate, value, and assimilate their understanding of life into a coherent social structure. Despite all of the scholarly books and theories that I had read by so called Afro-centric theorists, I was no closer to understanding and relating to people who looked so much like myself, yet saw and experienced the world so differently.

My initial professional considerations in moving to Africa were to act as a mediator between East African customers and US companies. However, after spending only a few months there, I began to see that this would be a tediously difficult task at best. Most US companies are completely ignorant of African economic structures, with the possible exceptions of South Africa or Egypt. The level of corruption both perceived and real is almost unimaginable to the average Westerner's mind. As a naive, young, idealistic journalist, was I in store for a rude awakening!

Before leaving to come to Tanzania, I had briefly spoken with several small and midsize medical supply companies and offered them potential growth in a new market. Initially, they seemed interested, as long as there was a guarantee of payments made before any of the goods would be shipped. There was a third component that I had overlooked; the exuberant cost of shipping from the United States to any port of entry into Africa. After inquiring around some of the local hospitals, it became clearly apparent that there was a lack of funds on the Tanzanian side. I had to make some severe adjustments. I notified my host family that I would be going on a small adventure by bus to investigate other areas of the country.

That was my first real excursion within Africa. I went to the local bus station in Dar Es Salaam and experienced intense cultural shock. The level of disorganization, confusion, and outright chaos was appalling! I must admit that it was one of the few times on my trip that I felt genuine fear. However, in retrospect, it was my sense of western order that was being challenged as opposed to my having been in any real or tangible danger. As I approached the purchase window to buy a ticket, I vividly recall the man behind the counter being both hostile and aloof. It took him almost four minutes before he would even look up to acknowledge my presence. He asked a question in a muffled form of Kiswahili, and I immediately let him know that I only spoke English. He then turned to the equally unfriendly female attendant on his right side, under his breath, I heard him murmur, "Black American." The female attendant asked, "where will you be traveling to?" I answered, "North to Arusha. How long will the trip take?"

Without ever looking up, she mumbled, "5,000 shillings, (equivalent to five US dollars at the time), and the trip will take over nine hours."

29

I thought that this would be a good way for me to view the country, relax, and also give me some time to restructure my consultant strategy. It was 11 a.m. when I purchased the ticket. The bus, scheduled to leave at 1 p.m., didn't arrive until 3 p.m. and didn't leave the road until 4 p.m. Unfortunately, time delays seemed to be the standard in Tanzania. Many of my fellow patrons (Tanzanians, of course) took the delay as though it were to be expected. I soon realized that my inner frustration was to no avail and that I was better off going with the flow. In reality, I didn't have any definitive time to be in any place.

It was liberating when I began to take a more laid-back approach because the ride ahead was extremely challenging. Unbeknownst to me was the fact that I had purchased a ticket for a chicken bus. (This is the name for any of the various local buses that run throughout East Africa.) The name comes from the fact that the locals often take chickens, food, and other livestock on board, sometimes as a means of feeding their families, often times as a way of supplementing their incomes. The seats were uncomfortable, and the bus was absurdly crowded. There was virtually no room for one to the arm or leg, and the aisles were covered with grain, vegetables, and other perishable goods. As we drove off into the night, I began to think of home and the comforts of Greyhound and other luxury bus lines in the USA. I reminisced over the smooth paved highways and efficiency of the transportation infrastructure back home. As the nightfall approached, the noise seemed to get louder and louder, and the bumps seemed to increase due to the driver's inability to measure the distance in front of him. His incessant honking of the horn, which was irritating at best, confused me. There was an older man of East Indian extraction who sat next to me. He opened the conversation. "Hello, are you American?"

"Yes," I smiled and gave him a bewildered look.

"My name is Ahmed and my family is originally from Goa, a Portuguese domain in India."

He must have taken notice of my nervousness and assured me that the honking of the bus horn was standard here in Tanzania and was done to prevent accidents since most drivers here enjoy passing in the speeding lane with almost reckless abandon. Obviously, this didn't ease my tension, as I then noticed that the driver was incessantly chewing on some strange odd-shaped green plant.

Ahmed would later explain, "This is a stimulant plant called *morah*, which is totally legal throughout East Africa. Most of the bus drivers here chew it to avoid fatigue."

That certainly didn't make me feel any less uneasy; the bus driver was basically driving high! Again, I quickly came to the realization that there was little I could do to change the situation.

As we moved north, it seemed that the bus would make local stops every twenty minutes or so. We were stopped by the police at least seven times, as I would later find out, because the police make so little, it was a actually an acceptable practice for them to take bribes in order to make ends meet and take care of their families. I sat back and became more engrossed in the conversation with Ahmed. He stated that he was on his way back from Zimbabwe. I was very surprised and asked him why Zimbabwe, with all of the political trouble that had taken place recently. He told me that doing business in Africa is about knowing how to spot the most opportunistic business opportunities. He said this is how business is done in Africa, and that the vultures acquire the lion's share here. He went on to say that it's much easier to buy cheap land, building contracts, and other goods when a country is going through an economic downturn such as Zimbabwe. I pondered on this for a while, and I then concluded that his statement made sense. It was similar to the process of buying a stock when the value is underrated. What goes up must come down.

He went on to tell me more details about himself. My first impression of him was that he was a local hustler who was a jack of all trades and a master of none. "my brother and I own a small trucking company in Arusha that specializes in shipping different goods to diverse parts of Eastern and Southern Africa. I am in the middle to setting up a deal that would deliver corn products from Tanzanian farms to buyers in Zimbabwe and Zambia." Both countries were experiencing droughts during this time.

"I have a sister who lives in upstate New York with her husband." He was very keen on going to the United States one day and was curious to know what I thought of Africa thus far. I told him that it was much too early to make any insightful analysis, although it was surely becoming a baptism by fire! As we continued our journey, we made a road stop at a local side restaurant for the bus to refuel and some of the passengers to stretch out and use the restroom. The first thing that I noticed was how aggressively flirtatious Ahmed was towards the local African women. Although I wasn't very conversant in Kiswahili, I was able to read between the lines and guess at the nuances. Flirting between the sexes is pretty universal.

The act of Ahmed's flirting wasn't off-putting in itself. However, his advances seemed to be directed only towards the local black African women. He conveniently ignored the small number of Asian women who were on the bus. Maybe this was simply a cultural dynamic that I didn't understand. Shortly after returning to our journey on the bus, I began to doze off into a semi-conscious sleep, finally getting acclimated to the bumpy road, uncomfortable seats, foul smell, and the reckless style of driving. As daylight began to break, I could see an enormous dark image over the horizon, resembling a great storm cloud. Ahmed pointed it out to me and told me that it was the great Mountain Kilimanjaro. As the sun began to rise to the east, I could make the mountain out more clearly. It was truly monumental, such an impressive display of nature rising out of the flat plains of northern Tanzania. It was almost surreal. All of the books, movies, and stories do so little to describe the sheer magnitude and beauty of the mountain. It truly looked like a stairway to heaven appearing from seemingly nowhere, shrouded in ancient mythos and inexplicable majesty. In my mind, it was as if all the tales, history, puzzles, and questions of Africa both modern and ancient, could be found somehow on the majestic heights of Kilimanjaro. To me, she was the ultimate symbol of the potential for which all of Africa could reach, the great vision of the future in which the ex-President, Julius Nyerere, would light a candle symbolizing the Swahili concept of *uhuru* or freedom. This trip was showing me that freedom is a very expensive ideal to achieve, and it usually starts from the inside. As is often the case, ideology and reality are often paradoxical ends of the spectrum, two ships that often miss each another in the night.

It was early morning when our bus finally pulled into the dusty town of Arusha. Ahmed invited me to stay with him and his family. I politely declined. I didn't want to inconvenience them or myself for the sake of him just being culturally polite. He insisted. "I would like to show you around the town since you are a guest here."

I went back to his home which was located on the outskirts of the city. He then led me through a narrow, damp alley to a small dark corridor on top of a small grocery shop. As we made our way to the third floor, the interior space became larger, resembling an odd-shaped hotel of sorts. We entered through a large wooden door which had multiple locks. After a couple of knocks, an older lady with a very disarming smile opened the door. Ahmed introduced her as his mother, Mrs. Desouza. She smiled and then asked me to sit. Ahmed and his mother began to speak in a language that I didn't recognize. I awkwardly sat there hoping that I wasn't the center of their conversation. After a few minutes, it became very evident that I was, although she was doing everything in her power to conceal it. After ten minutes of intense conversation between Ahmed and her, he stated, "I am going downstairs to fetch some more groceries for the evening meal."

This gave his mother the opportunity to interrogate me, all under the guise of getting to know me better. She asked, "which state in the US did you come from?"

"New Jersey," I answered.

She immediately began to warm up to me. "My daughter lives in upstate New York, Buffalo, and I spent five months visiting there." She told me about the brief time she spent in Atlantic City. I interrupted her and mentioned that this was my city of birth. We both laughed in a way that implied a shared knowledge and perhaps a spark of trust.

"I was greatly relieved to find out that you're from the US as opposed to somewhere in Africa!" I was taken aback and felt slightly insulted, so I asked her why she felt that way.

"My son Ahmed is very naïve, and there is a substantial influx of Nigerian drug dealers looking to set up shop in Tanzania. I worry day and night that he will get involved with the wrong type of business person and eventually get himself in a lot of trouble."

To me, this seemed like a sure sign of racism. The insinuation that non-Africans were less likely to exhibit criminal tendencies was highly insulting and offensive. The paradox was that Ahmed and his mother were being very warm and hospitable to me on a personal basis, one of the many contradictions of living in Tanzania. Many countries in Africa can surely be said to be the tale of two cities, one rich in minerals, gems, natural resources, and more importantly warm everlasting family relations, both with the living and dead. On the other hand, there is extreme poverty in many of its countries, poverty in its educated and skilled human labor force, poverty in its infrastructure and its health care and educational institutions, and more importantly in many of its leaders' moral values. This combination often makes for very strange bedfellows, creating a wide field of opportunity for economic exploiters, opportunists, and others who don't have Africa's best intentions at heart to come in and prosper.

This manifests in a myriad of ways, from the economic domination by Asian Indians in East Africa, to the inequitable relationship of many international NGO's about the African governments which they claim to want to help, as well as many other exploitive relationships. The deeper one looks here, one will find that things are not always what they appear to be. During my earlier experiences with African religions back in the US, it was very clear that there were very little distinctions made between good and evil, God and the devil, and the spirit and matter. These very concepts of the ancestors existing amongst the living helped me to understand to some degree the paradoxical African logic. Every setback seemed to hold a seed of creation, every negative experience seemed to hold a window of redemption, and every severe human conflict seemed to hold the magic potential of compassionate reconciliation. It was certainly the case in

Tanzania, the land of sweeping contradictions, that seemingly opposing forces could be reconciled and perhaps someday comprehended.

Later that evening, Ahmed's mother cooked the best sausage that I have ever tasted in my life. She said, "this is a special creation of my Goan culture." I told her that I was interested to know more about the history of her culture.

"We originally came from the southwestern part of India that was colonized by the Portuguese. We differ from other Indians in having Portuguese surnames, and being strong Catholics. The majority of Asian Indians living in East Africa are Gujarat speakers."

This surely set the Goans apart, not only from their fellow black Africans but also from other Indian ethnic groups in East Africa. This was one of the many unique formations that international colonization and inter-global movements brought to Africa.

Ahmed returned shortly to the apartment with a large selection of vegetables, meats, and a corn-based staple known as *ugali*. Mrs. Desouza asked me, "do you know Peter and Charlotte O'Donnell?" I asked her who they were, and she said that they were expatriate black Americans who lived in Tanzania for years. She also mentioned that they used to be involved in the pork-selling industry but now run a local NGO about twelve miles outside of town. I said I would be interested in meeting them. I was really excited to meet fellow Afro-Americans this far away from home. A million thoughts were running through my mind. How did they come here? How were they able to adjust to a place that was so different from the USA?

Waking up at dawn, (I always found it hard to sleep late in Africa), it seemed that everyone and everything would rise with the sun. The cackling of roosters, the shuffling of people all seemingly in concert, and the smell of firewood burning in the early morning mist; these simple happenings would forever be ingrained in my mind. The mornings in Africa will never be forgotten. Ahmed stated that the best way to see the O'Donnells would be at the market downtown. We went around to some of the local vegetable markets. Ahmed spoke to a couple of the locals who seemed confused at first when he mentioned the name, Peter O'Donnell. One young man with dark skin contrasting his white teeth at first looked perplexed and then smiled and said, "oh you mean Rasta–man?" I was taken off guard a little, as Ahmed explained to me that Peter wore dreadlocks in his hair. In Tanzania, anyone with this type of hairstyle is automatically considered a Rastafarian. We both laughed for a moment and then resumed our walk around the town. Arusha was a small dusty town in comparison to the capital Dar Es Salaam. However, there were a couple of things that distinguished it from other cities in Tanzania. It was headquarters to the new United Nations Commission on Human Rights based on the Rwandan genocide. It was here that President Clinton claimed the city to be the Switzerland of Africa. It is also the town that many foreigners transferred into game parks of northern Tanzania. Lastly, this was one of the two major towns from where Mount Kilimanjaro could be seen.

We walked for more than an hour, crossing a small polluted stream filled with loose garbage and dry mud. The water seemed to divide the city, separating the less affluent part of town from the more prosperous area filled with expats. Most of the wealthier community worked for the new and growing United Nations base in Arusha. I came to detect an attitude of entitlement and exclusivity. Vivid memories of upscale neighborhoods back home projected into my imagination. As my mind began to simply wander,

I was almost oblivious to the white van that pulled up beside Ahmed and myself. It was playing some of the most soothing traditional American jazz that I've heard in a long time. Shortly after, a man stepped out of the van with long flowing gray dreadlocks, a pepper-colored goatee, and bright blue traditional African pants and shirt. He immediately made his presence known to the young vegetable seller by speaking a broken version of Kiswahili in a loud southern accent. I immediately identified him as an Afro-American before Ahmed had the chance to point him out. I waited a couple of minutes before being introduced. The first words to come out of Peter's mouth were, "It's a pleasure to meet you, sir!"

I identified myself as a fellow Afro-American from New Jersey. He smiled and stated, "brother, I'm from Kansas."

We each chuckled. I told him that I was a big fan of Jazz and asked him which song he was listening to. He commented that it was Charlie Parker. I stated how appropriate it was being from Kansas. He invited me to come inside his van and take a look. The van was fully equipped with a bar, television, and soft leather couches. This scene was very out of place in Tanzania! *Wow,* I was thinking, *finally a taste of home.* Peter invited me back to the village to meet his wife and other members of his non-profit organization. I was delighted to meet fellow Afro-Americans that were living the diasporan experience outside the USA. Pete's story was more amazing than I could have ever imagined!

As we approached the village, which was located twenty minutes outside of downtown Arusha, I observed older women dressed in traditional clothes carrying different goods on their heads with a natural effortless elegance. Many of the young children were running up and down the dirt road, carrying large buckets of water that they fetched from a local stream nearby. As we left the van, several children running nearby suddenly slowed down, dropped their eyes, and said the word *shikamoo*. At first I really didn't understand the significance of this. However, Peter quickly explained that this was a form of respect that was cross-generational. Children would say *shikamoo*, a Kiswahili phrase of respect to their elders, and in response, we were supposed to answer this with *madahaba*. He explained that this tradition wasn't limited to interaction between young children and adults, but it also extended to the relationship between younger adults and those persons considered their elders. Once again I saw how this African cosmology, which I first learned about through the African-based religions in the US, seemed to permeate many levels of traditional African life, even if on a subconscious level. This traditional cosmology, which places such tremendous reference and esteem between the relationship of one's family, community, and its ancestors, like anything else also has negative and positive results. As is often the case, these two opposing synergies often play out in such proximity that one gets confused in the ability to separate the two. Later that afternoon, Peter introduced me to everyone in the compound. The first person to come out was his wife, Charlotte O'Donnell. She was better known as Mama Charlotte. She was a very imposing woman, standing around 5'10", stout yet soft and feminine at the same time. She had a beautiful caramel complexion and a warm and engaging smile. She spoke with a soft Southern accent. However, her eyes had a fiery determination in them. Mama Charlotte was also a talented artist. She showed me some of her paintings and sculptures which were nothing short of breathtaking, revealing a heightened sense of intuition and wisdom in her artwork. Although born and raised in the United States, her artwork reflected the soul of Africa in them. Later after learning more about her life, I would understand how and why her work reflected such an intense cultural connection to the continent.

The next person in the compound who I was introduced to was Debra, affectionately known as Deb. She was a former journalist of Irish descent from the New England area in her mid-40s, a seemingly established woman who one day just up and left everything and moved to Tanzania to volunteer at Peter O'Donnell's NGO. I felt that this was very strange, and I wondered what caused a woman who was fairly established in her life to decide to make such a dramatic life change. This was actually quite admirable. Here, an American-born and raised, white, middle-aged female from a relatively privileged background came to the middle of Africa to work as a volunteer! This seemed like a very selfless act at the time. Strange but admirable. Deb was in charge of teaching English for Peter's NGO. She helped to deliver free books from the United States and dispersed them among the village schools. She was also quite adept with computers and IT in general. Having someone with those skills was surely a great asset to Peter's organization. I was then introduced to the local Tanzanians, many of whom lived in the compound and attended the local classes.

That evening Mama Charlotte showed me to my room, which was actually not a room at all, but rather a small self-contained compound, with its own bathroom, sink, and dresser. The last words out of her mouth were, "please shut the door tight because cobras have a tendency to come in looking for rats!"

Luckily for them or me, I didn't have a phobia for snakes, but I could only imagine my father's reaction in the same situation! I took a nice lukewarm shower and then made my way down to the dinner quarters. At the large dining table, I was finally able to get Peter to open up about his reasons for coming to Africa. He began his story by telling me that he had been in Africa for over thirty years. He came in 1972 to escape a conviction that was sentenced by a racist judge in Kansas. Peter stated that he used to be in charge of the Kansas chapter of the Black Panthers; a black nationalist group formed in Oakland, California, during the late '60s-early '70s. He stated, "I was charged with running guns across state lines." Because of the FBI's secret war on black groups called COINTELPRO, which basically gave both local and federal law enforcement the right to use any means necessary to dismantle or kill so-called militant groups. Peter received a life sentence. Because of a threat by a local Kansas Sheriff, who told him, "boy you're going to jail but you ain't never coming out alive," he decided to skip bail and live overseas in exile.

"My wife Charlotte and I were just beginning to date at that time; I was thirty-three, and she was only nineteen. I broke the news to her that I was leaving the country and going into exile. She turned to me and said, 'I am going into exile with you.' I was in disbelief. Charlotte was always stubborn, and I loved her that much more for it." By contacting the international chapter of the Black Panther Party, Peter and Mama Charlotte were sent to Paris, disguised as an international journalist and his devoted wife. Peter said, "I was in a hotel room speaking to a European journalist from Spain. He stated that he recalled a magazine article written on the Afro-American photojournalist named Gordon Parks." Mama Charlotte recalled that moment. "I had to stop Peter in the middle of his performance because the story had become so far-fetched." We all burst out laughing. "From France, Mama Charlotte and I made our way to Algeria, which at the time was the international headquarters of the Black Panther Party." One of the most ironic things that happened when they arrived in Algeria was that one of the leaders of the Panther Party angrily asked him, "where the hell have you been? Your mother has been looking for you!"

We again laughed together. "Young brother, Southern hospitality even extends all the way to Algeria." He told me these were some of the many small things that he missed being away from home. I was genuinely intrigued and fascinating by their life story. Two Afro-Americans exiled out of the United States and salvaged in noble Africa! As Peter began to talk more in depth about his exile, he let me know that this had been a very hard choice for him to make. "At the time Algeria claimed itself to be a revolutionary socialist country. Because the Black Panthers declared themselves social revolutionaries, they found political amnesty here as there was no extradition treaty with the United States."

Mama Charlotte and Peter shared their individual perspectives on the living conditions. They each stated that the Algerians, both Arabs and Berbers, where terribly racist!

Mama Charlotte stated, "Algerian men would often make sexually provocative gestures towards me without giving a second thought, assuming that both black and American women have loose morals."

"After spending almost a year in Algeria, our stay ended when an alleged member of the Black Panther Party was accused of dating an Algerian woman." I was told that in many Arab nations, Western women were perceived as easy, while Arab women were held above reproach, especially to foreign non-Islamic men.

"In this hostile environment, we decided to leave North Africa and head for Tanzania at the invitation of a good friend."

During this time, Tanzania was also a socialist country, but it was part of a different region of Africa than was Algeria. Julius Nyerere was a black pan-Africanist who believed that the freedom of one African country was connected to all African countries. He was one of the few leaders who actually practiced what he preached, from the beginning of his presidency to his voluntary retirement from politics. It was in Tanzania that Peter and Mama Charlotte would truly find both a safe haven and cultural refuge from the constant alienation and political pressure they each faced since their escape from the United States.

During the independence campaign of the 1950s, Julius Nyerere and his Tanganyika African National Union (TANU) political movement invoked a very important symbolism of Tanzanian nationalism based on the famous rebellion named Maji Maji. This rebellion broke out in the Southern region of Tanzania in 1905, named after the *maji* water medicine that many Tanzanian fighters believed would give them immunity to German colonial bullets. The rebellion was started by local village headmen who had become caught between unfair German monetary policies and local villagers who bore the brunt of colonial rule.

German colonial rulers and their appointed African/Arab helpers required many of the village leaders to work on their estates for virtually no compensation. The Germans also prevented the Tanzanians from using the forest as a means of making a living. The effects of these severe laws helped to slow down African agricultural production and self-sufficiency. Many of the village leaders who refused to implement this racist and destructive policies were jailed or killed.

The rebellion was planned about a year in advance under the leadership and guidance of spirit mediums who helped to distribute medicine water as well as African spies to help flame the revolt among neighboring groups. When the fighting did break out, most tribal leaders were well prepared to take up arms. The actual fighting began in the southern part of the Matumbi Hills where African fighters attacked a local German garrison. As word of the uprising spread, African rebels organized their troops to assault any reflection of German colonial rule, including Arab and Indian traders, askari police and soldiers, German settlers and missionaries, and of course German trading posts. In Tanzania, Maji Maji was the first concerted rebellion to German colonial rule.

Africans armed with muskets, spears, and arrows encountered German forces made up of mostly Arab/African askari troops commanded by German officers. While most of the fighting was over within a few months, many rebel leaders held out for two years. In many areas, Germans burned villages and field crops, confiscated food, raped and took many African women hostage to prevent them from aiding rebels. As a result of these strategies, thousands of African civilians died through famine and dislocation. German officials put the record of African casualties at 70,000, while unofficial oral records put the figure closer to over 250,000.

Although the goal of the Maji Maji rebellion to officially end German colonial rule failed, Germany's colonial policy in Africa underwent drastic changes and would never be the same. Most scholars view the Maji Maji as a break between an era that blindly accepted European/German colonial privileges. The German plantations and settlers had to work now with a free labor market. After the rebellion, forced labor was no longer accepted anywhere in the colony. Following the Maji Maji uprising, German officials confronted the influence of indigenous African religious expression and spirit mediums as they were viewed as being sparks of dissent to European rule. This allowed Islam and Christianity to fill the roles of cultural and religious leadership in many East African nations.

Citing the Maji Maji uprising as the first example of concerted inter-tribal Tanzanian resistance to colonial rule, Julius Nyerere and his political party TANU depicted themselves as heirs to this early anti-colonial movement. Within this rich and sensitive cultural heritage, Peter and Mama Charlotte would settle and build a life.

It seems that the Afro-American living both home and abroad has been thrusted into the essence of this hunger for closure and has responded in a diversity of ways that testify to our unique formation in slavery and displacement (or alienation) and self-restoration through a humanistic ethos that sometimes appears to be a deliberate act of faith; more of a subconscious yearning than a cultural given. To me, Peter and Charlotte O'Donnell seemed to exemplify this quest or vision for not only cultural integrity but also social and political restitution.

I was a guest on the compound for over a week. The one distinguishing feature about Arusha is its somewhat dreary climate, at least in comparison to Dar Es Salaam, which is a sunny coastal city. One evening after returning to my room, I realized that I had been in Arusha for almost over two weeks and had yet to see Mount Kilimanjaro. This majestic mountain, which held such a fascination for me in childhood, seemed to be almost nonexistent. How ironic? Here I was no more than forty miles from this monumental symbol, and I was unable to even get a glimpse of her majesty. The next morning around 6 a.m. I received a loud knock on my door. I jumped up and opened it, and then realized that it was Debbie. She told me in a most urgent voice, "hurry up and get dressed; Kili is out, you can see her from the southwest corner of the yard!" Kili is short for Mount Kilimanjaro. I quickly washed up, threw on my jeans and a sweatshirt, and ran as fast as i could to catch my second glance of the highest mountain in Africa. As I gazed upon her magic for the second time, it became apparent to me for the first time just how far away from home I was. The reality of the distance really hit me and for a brief moment, I felt a strange sense of loneliness and melancholy. This was the opposite effect that the mountain had on me the first time, yet the two feelings were somehow interconnected, strangely related on some subconscious primordial level it seemed. Debra and I sat there in the brisk Arusha morning and pondered our own personal thoughts in the midst of this snow-capped Queen, which has been written about by authors such as Ernest Hemingway and others. It was also worshiped by local tribes such as the Chagga. We stood so closely and yet I was left with such conflicting and distant emotions. As I looked over at Debra, my confusion was transformed into suspense as I wondered what thoughts were going through her mind. I wondered what secrets she held from her previous life in New England, what dreams or nightmares had brought her on this journey across the Atlantic into the heart of the Dark Continent. Although she had a very disarming demeanor, there was sadness in her eyes. A deep grief engulfed her aura. When she spoke, there seemed to be a mask of pain that she was trying to hide, a dark secret she was keeping that maybe she thought Africa could heal, could transform, or could somehow make her forget. I didn't want to probe. There was a subtle tone in her voice which seemed to want to share this pain, letting the world know what she had gone through and sacrificed to come and selflessly volunteer in this part of the world.

I guess deep down inside there is some primordial need for us as human beings to focus on the trials and tribulations of others in order to soften or maybe diminish our own pain and failures. I wondered if coming to Africa fed my own subconscious need by exposing me to a surface condition of people who appeared to be living in much worse society than myself. As I sat there in the midst of this mighty mountain, my thoughts alternated between Debra's story and my own personal motivations. The perception that we agreed upon was that living in Tanzania always reduces the constant feeling of isolation and individualism that one will unquestionably feel while living in the States. The entire communal culture permeates everything here, leaving it virtually impossible to feel disconnected from people or community. Many Westerners are often overwhelmed at the amount of social attention that they receive when they visit Sub-Saharan Africa, some of it sincere and much of it not! Like many of the things that a Westerner must adapt to both culturally and socially, it takes patience, courage, and open-mindedness to be able to adjust and acclimate oneself into the gross and subtle differences that African culture can have on a person from the West. In retrospect, I can say that I've never felt more challenged, more creative, and more alive than when I was adjusting my reality to living in Africa. There was always a sense of surrealism; somehow reality and make-belief connected at a duration point that was always absent from my reality in the States or even Europe for that matter. Maybe this had to do with the fact that most of Sub-Saharan Africa were going through an identity crisis. It was not sure if it wanted to be Western, Arabic, or African. Then one may ask, what is African? This last question would perplex me for my entire three years of living on the continent.

As we departed for our individual compounds that afternoon, we both left with a renewed sense of wonder and meaning as to why we had come to Africa. That evening was unusually cool even for the highlands of Arusha. Mama Charlotte announced that two special friends were coming from the lakeside town of Mwanza in northwestern Tanzania. Mama Charlotte spoke extremely high of the new guests and was really going out of her way to make sure that the compound was properly prepared for their arrival. I must admit that I didn't share their enthusiasm. The Tanzanians that I had met thus far had been somewhat of a disappointment. Maybe this was an unfair judgment based on my slightly different expectations and values. Nevertheless, this is how I felt, and only time would tell if my feelings would match the reality of my perceptions.

That evening, the volunteer staff cooked a huge feast. We all contributed to setting up the large dining area located at the back of the compound. The dining area was spacious, and it overlooked the thick bushes which seemed to become more mysterious at night, holding secrets that the African earth would never reveal easily. It was unique in that everything was set up like an American Jazz club back home. Peter had pictures of famous jazz musicians such as Charlie Parker, his favorite because of the Kansas connection, Miles Davies, and John Coltrane. There was a pair of boxing gloves hung up over the built-in fireplace/stove. I can remember the familiar smell of barbecued meat, soul food, with the sounds of traditional American Jazz playing, yet when I looked outside into the thick dark woods which seem to go on forever, I was instantly reminded of where I was. It was a very strange mixture of being close to something that was so familiar and looking outwardly at something so distant and foreign.

After two hours, Bill and Jimmie finally arrived. They were not what I expected. In fact, my perception was totally wrong. First of all, they were not Tanzanian but African Americans. It was very evident from the beginning that Jimmie, the wife, was the most gregarious of the two. She came in and greeted everyone in the Kiswahili greeting *asante saana*, which means hello. Both of them had a very warm and welcoming aura. Jimmie was petite with beautiful brown skin which seemed almost ethereal when looking at her from certain angles. She spoke with a very measured but confident tone. Bill, on the other hand, was reticent and seemed almost content playing second fiddle to his wife. He was very fair-skinned with a slight build; so thin that he seemed almost anorexic. This was surely the dynamic of a non-Tanzanian relationship or any African one for that matter. As we all sat down at the evening meal, Debra asked Jimmie how she and her husband were fairing with their missionary post work in Mwanza. Mwanza is a large city located in the northwest section of the country on the banks of the famous Lake Victoria. Jimmie replied that things were going well. However, they decided to end their contract the following year and return to the States. They had lived almost twelve years of their lives in Africa and wanted to spend some time with their newly born grandchild back in New York. I asked them what originally brought them to Africa. Jimmie quietly smiled, looked at Mama Charlotte, and kindly asked me, "young brother, how much time do you have?" I looked back at her and stated that the night was still young, and aside from going to sleep, I had no place to be. She began to tell me that she and her husband Bill had come to Tanzania back in 1972. They were young, idealistic, and looking to make a difference in a developing country that seemed to share their global vision. Bill finally then came out of his shell and spoke about how they had come with a group of young progressive African Americans looking for an alternative to the American way of life. They wanted to share their skills, knowledge, and expertise in a land that seemed to need it; a land that appeared to be on the verge of creating an authentic African community, based on traditional indigenous principles.

Jimmie took a deep breath and looked up at the sky with an almost reminiscent look in her eyes, a look that relayed a sense of joy conveyed with the profound wisdom of one who has learned a valuable lesson by going through the trials and tribulations of life. Jimmie spoke softly and stated that their first years in Tanzania were extremely difficult. Both Bill and Jimmie received work as teachers at a local school in Arusha. At that point, Jimmie blurted out a thunderous contagious laugh. She went on to say that the working conditions were deplorable, pay was almost non-existent, however, there was a sense of mission, purpose, accomplishment in working in these challenging conditions, and the rich fulfillment of making tremendous differences in the lives of young Tanzanian students. I could understand this deep commitment to finding some sense of purpose outside the often mundane middle-class American dream of simply making more money. There is an African saying that a tree must understand its roots in order for it to grow. In listening to these elder Afro- American activists, it was I who was a branch and learning from the past experiences of those who came before me. Listening to their stories gave me great insight into my own motivations, my own shadows, and my own passions. It was like looking into a mirror of the future. There was a great amount of wisdom springing from the well of experiences of these elders. It's strange how I traveled thousands of miles from home only to be brought back in its shadow, then return to its roots and essence. These are some of the paradoxes of living in Africa. Looking for one experience, I found an entirely different way of seeing the problem.

That night it was hard to sleep. I recall the sounds of heavy raindrops falling on the roof of my small compound, along with the crisp wind fearlessly howling during the midnight hour. I lay awake that evening and vividly visualized everything that Jimmie had told us. I imagined myself in the past with them, and for a brief moment, I could almost feel the magic of wonder, adventure, and sense of mission. It must have been a great feeling to know that they were there during such a great time of change. The sky must have seemed like the limit then. As I dozed off that night, my idealism was rudely awakened by the familiar sounds of chickens roosting in the wee hours of the morning. I looked over at my watch and realized that I had a yoga appointment in fifteen minutes with Billie and Jimmie. I begrudgingly got out of bed and went into the shower stall to turn on the lukewarm water. I really wasn't interested in doing yoga, but I figured that since we were all guests why not be polite and try something different, at least for one time.

We all met in the large compound which was positioned in the front of the yard. As I arrived, Billie, Mama Charlotte, Debra, Jimmie, and a new guest, Joji, greeted me! I was a little taken back by Joji's presence which was totally unexpected. As Jimmie began to sit in her yoga pose getting everyone in the room to stretch and breathe synchronically, I found it difficult to concentrate due to my strong and overwhelming attraction to Joji. She was very slender, about 5'7" to 5'8" in height, with a smooth golden honey complexion and hazel eyes. She gave me a warm, if somewhat aloof, smile in which she revealed a set of perfectly white teeth. I would later find out that her full name was Joji Cleaver. Daughter of the late Eldridge and Kathleen Cleaver, both of whom were major icons within the Black Panther Party. She was soft-spoken, elegant, and slender. Although she had her mother's fair complexion and narrow features, her father lived through her eyes. She had the same harmonic cat-like eyes that hid a fire and passion like her father Eldridge Cleaver had expressed during his turbulent and committed life.

Joji was a living example of a very ancient African parable, which states that our ancestors live through us and in us. Looking at her was like looking back in time, looking at the early struggles of the Civil Rights movement, feeling the raw, youthful passion and idealism of revolutionary zeal.

Moments later, I returned to my yoga workout and tried to focus on the movements that Jimmie was trying to relay. In an instant, I was able to feel a slight discomfort in what seemed like a very simple poise. At that moment, I realized that there might be something more to this ancient Indian practice than I had initially thought. We continued with different yoga postures for another forty minutes and ended with a very relaxing meditation session. As I sat there in the lotus pose, a standard yoga pose for meditation, I tried to prevent my thoughts from running in every direction. Thinking how crazy it was that I came thousands of miles to East Africa to learn how to do yoga! How ironic it was that I was in the heart of Tanzania embracing an ancient Indian philosophy and lifestyle.

After yoga practice, we all congregated in the dining compound to eat breakfast. I observed something special, a synergy that I'd always pondered but had never experienced for myself. I looked across the large wooden dining table and observed Mama Charlotte staring at Peter, and at that moment I saw for the first time what real love looked like and what true companionship could be. After breakfast, I leaned over and quietly asked her if she was still in love with Peter. She smiled in an almost girlish manner and shyly shook her head yes. I was elated. It was like discovering something that I'd always believed existed, but somehow it remained elusive, never allowing me to find its tangible expression. I asked her how that was possible, how they were able to keep the flame of passion and commitment alive after so many years of being together. Speaking with her slightly Southern drawl, she said that she believed that their love was able to grow, mature, and endure because of their deep commitment to a larger struggle, to their higher vision of creating good for the community at large. She observed that many marriages and relationships in the US are consumed with self-centered motives, and she stated that true love can't operate on a small scale superficial level. She believed that for love to flourish and flow like a river, it must be based on something greater than the individual self, that it must be more expensive than one person's immediate selfish desires and needs. This one conversation would forever change my concept of what constitutes a successful relationship.

My romantic sights were now focused on Joji. She was beautiful, intelligent, the daughter of a revolutionary, and a seemingly dedicated pan-Africanist! In my mind, I thought this was surely fate. I imagined that maybe after some years of being together we would have our own adventure stories about doing development work in distant lands.

A few hours later, my little fantasy world came to abrupt ending when another surprise guest entered the compound. It was no other than Geronimo Pratt. He was an ex-Black Panther activist made famous by Johnny Cochran, who successfully defended his release from San Quentin State Prison after years of incarceration based upon false charges by the state of California. He was a lot smaller in person than he appeared on television, with a shiny bald head, a black-and-white-pepper mustache, and surprisingly kind eyes. He had a very laid-back Southern demeanor and spoke with a low tone rich with Louisianian gentility. I was expecting him to have a much harder outer edge. After he sat down and started to talk, one could immediately sense the profound aura of inner strength and focus that he possessed. There seemed to be a deep sense of self, a centeredness of a man who has seen and survived the worst that life has to offer and now was ready to take his place in the sun. His advanced age, 56, automatically precluded in my mind the chances of romance between him and her. Later that evening, to everyone's surprise, Geronimo and Joji announced that they were married. My romantic hopes, regardless of how brief, had suddenly disappeared in a flash.

That evening, I lay in my small sleeping compound and pondered deeply on why Joji would marry a man almost twice her age? A man who was so close to her father that he would be considered an uncle-type figure. Two things entered my mind; the first was the obvious factor that she missed her father and wanted to reproduce the love and intimacy that may have been neglected because of his revolutionary lifestyle. By marrying a man that was not only close to her father in age, but also in his philosophical and political leanings, she may have consciously or subconsciously tried to recapture that relationship.

My next thought was not so noble or romantic. It was a retraction to the notion of materialism and blatant manipulation of feminine wiles in order to achieve materialistic goals. Maybe she was only after his money? It was no secret that Geronimo, with the help of Johnny Cochran, had won a substantial amount of money from the state of California. I then immediately questioned my own motive in thinking so negatively about it. If the two of them were happy and in love then more power to them! At that moment, I felt a deep sense of relief. For the first time, I was able to detach myself truly from my own thinking and judgments and sit back and observe the observer in a sense. Instead of judging Joji and Geronimo's situation, I needed to question my own motives and try to understand why their relationship made me feel a tad uncomfortable.

I thought of an earlier conversation between myself and Jimmie in which she'd stated, "Yoga was not only a physical regiment but also a philosophic approach to life, a different way of viewing the world." It was yoga's deep commitment to self-analysis that had really made an impression on me. This was the true beginning of my deep search for self-understanding. Instead of trying to comprehend this new society in which I was engaging myself, I also wanted to understand my motives and reactions fully while living this experience. Many people often create romantic notions based on their own internal measurements which often have very little to do with reality. I concluded that evening that I was projecting my need to find someone who would understand my intense need to travel into underdeveloped areas of the world, particularly Sub-Saharan Africa, and make a difference in the lives of the less fortunate. It was a yearning to find someone who could truly empathize with my burning passion for helping the underdog and to right the wrongs and injustices of this world, regardless of how far I'd have to travel, or what path I would have to take in order to find it.

In the back of my mind, I secretly nurtured this romantic inclination of my ideal partner like every other person does, whether he or she admits it or not.

The conversation between Mama Charlotte and myself really reconfirmed my belief that a couple must share a committed vision larger than themselves in order to build a solid, loving foundation. I guess my enthusiasm got the best of me when I first saw Joji. I thought this could be a sign of fate. I mean, what were the chances that I would meet a beautiful, intelligent, idealistic lady committed to social change in the middle of a village in Tanzania? At the end of the day, I was able to gain some sense of objectivity and clarity regarding my own personal motivations.

The next day, I went down to visit the United Nations building in downtown Arusha. The building was a huge elegant off-white color, which deeply contrasted with the rest of the downtown area. There seemed to be a constant gray cloud coming off the thick dust. This building housed the United Nations tribunal for the Genocide of Rwanda. Many people here believed that it was merely a political symbol to quench the guilt of the West's attitude of indifference and disinterest during the Rwandan genocide. I had mixed emotions on the issue. On one hand, I believed that it was a refreshing change to see the international community finally come together and give the proper acknowledgment of the tragic events which took place during this horrible act. On the other hand, it was almost a case of too little too late. There seemed to be a lot of political games going on according to locals, and the longer that the prosecution waited, the more obscure that the criminal cases would become.

As I approached a large black gate, a short dark-skinned security guard approached me. He stood about 5'5" and had a stocky built. The guard spoke English with a very strong African accent, which didn't immediately reveal his country of origin. I then greeted him with the Swahili *habare gani*, which is a somewhat informal way of saying hello throughout East Africa. A very warm smile received my greeting. I then extended my hand and stated, "my name is Hassan."

He responded, "my name is Mguni Ngeri. Where are you from?"

"From the USA. New Jersey to be exact!"

Mr. Mguni seemed instantly fascinated after hearing my country of origin. He told me that he was born and raised in the city of Mwanza, which is located in the Northwestern region of Tanzania; ironically this city is very close to the birth town of the late Julius Nyerere, the founding father of the nation.

Mr. Mguni then gave me an ID badge and escorted me to the office of procurement which was located on the third floor. As I moved up the old corridor, I was overwhelmed at the number of diverse accents being spoken. After approaching the main procurement office, several ladies were speaking French with a strong West African dialect. As we entered the room, I was overcome by the deep silence that was somewhat unnerving. For a brief moment, I was unsure if I should give a greeting in Swahili or French. I gave a half-hearted *bonjour*, and all the women responded to me with a very aloof bonjour, except the one lady who was sitting down.

She had a very warm smile and greeted me in Creolized French. She was a tall, dark, and stately-looking woman. Despite the fact that she was over six feet tall, there was an elegant femininity in her aura. She seemed to be very much at ease with herself, which made it effortless to approach her. I slowly sat down and introduced myself, stating, "hello my name is Hassan." She responded in kind, "My name is Kalifa." She gave me a warm smile. However, she was very deliberate in not extending out her hand. I wasn't surprised at the lack of gesture since I knew that customs between men and women in predominantly Muslim countries could vary. The shorter lady that was standing towards the door then asked me what I was doing in Tanzania. Although she seemed sincerely curious, there appeared to be an underlying resentment in her tone. I got the uneasy feeling that she wasn't completely happy with my presence. Nevertheless, I went on to answer her; I kept my answers very brief and professional. I told her that I was in Tanzania on business, working as a business correspondent, helping to facilitate and distribute medical supplies to the poorer population here. She gave me that same haughty slightly condescending smile. The smile seemed to project her profound indifference. I was left with a feeling that to her, what I was doing was not relevant or realistic.

There was an acute staleness that pervaded the entire building, reflecting a stoically bureaucratic institution. After what seemed to be half the day, but which was in reality perhaps no more than forty minutes to an hour later, I finally entered the procurement officer. She entered the waiting room and arrogantly called out my name in a very strong Caribbean accent. I answered   with a friendly smile only to be met by her suspicious eyes. She extended her hand out and casually stated that her name was Audrey. I got the feeling that her response was almost mechanical and she probably spent the better portion of her day greeting wealthy potential clients of the UN. She asked me in an almost matter of fact tone, "what are you doing in Tanzania?"

I stated, "this is my first time in Africa and I have always dreamed of visiting Tanzania." She gave me a very stern stare and then burst out laughing. She looked at me and very bluntly asked why in God's name, of all the places to visit in Africa, would I pick a place like Tanzania, which had only one movie theatre, virtually no shopping malls, and where time seemed to move backwards. I must admit that I was a little shocked to hear such negativity coming from the mouth of a UN worker, especially one of African descent!

I smiled and asked, "why are you living and working here then?"

She immediately rebutted. "I am certainly not living or working in Tanzania by choice. I would leave at the first given opportunity."

I then answered, "my purpose for coming to Tanzania was to find some of the purity of culture, some of the human principles that were left behind by President Julius Nyerere."

She just sat there and shook her head with disdainful contempt. She smirked. "One of the worst things that could have happened to Tanzania was Nyerere. He basically destroyed the economy with his unrealistic idealism."

I then looked around her office and saw a myriad of different photos, mostly of children. Since I have always been fascinated with photography, I proceeded to inquire about her photos.

As is typical of Caribbean culture, she was only too happy to oblige. She started with her siblings, whom all lived in Montreal, Canada. Of all the photos in the room, the one that caught my attention the most was a large picture of a very attractive young lady, maybe in her mid to late '20s, sitting on Audrey's desk. I couldn't help but show a vivid interest and Audrey immediately picked up on this. She smiled to herself and told me that the young lady that I was staring at was her niece and she was a lawyer living in Miami, Florida. I tried to look somewhat disinterested, however I've never been able to truly hide my intentions well.

Audrey glared at me and then asked," you're a handsome young man. Are you romantically involved with someone?"

I was a little taken aback by this, but nevertheless I just went along and answered, "my fiancé is back home in the USA waiting for me." She then asked, "what is wrong with her for allowing such a handsome man to travel such a long distance without her being present?" At this point, Audrey probably noticed my uneasiness and decided to abruptly change the conversation to her immediate family here in Arusha. I was very relieved not to have to continue with the third degree of my romantic life. She then continued describing her personal life, "I am a single mother of two adopted children."

I stated that adoption was one of the noblest things that a person could do. I then noted that back in the states, far too many Afro- Americans don't adopt. Audrey quietly agreed with me. "My eldest son was an HIV orphan from Zambia. My ex-husband and I were unsure if he was even going to live. We took the risk anyway based on our unbridled human emotion of raw compassion." The more she spoke, the more apparent it became that behind her harsh raspy exterior was a very compassionate, warm, almost insecure person. Her eyes seemed to hide an unspoken wound that had never healed.

As is often the case in Africa, I had to listen intently. Not only with my ears and mind, but with my deeper intuition. I yearned to hear or rather feel beyond the words, I learned to assess what wasn't being said. This would be one of many gifts that I received while living in Africa. As is the case with anything worthwhile, growing pains aren't always easily discernable in the beginning.

As the meeting came to an end, we summarized the possibilities of how I could write and perhaps contract with the UN. For the first time, the realization of my ambitions seemed to be manifesting. Previously, I was unsure of how I was even going to obtain a working news contract in a country as poor as Tanzania. For now however, there seemed to be some light at the end of the tunnel through my new contact Audrey, who was Head of Procurement and human resources. As I left, Audrey and I exchanged information and she told me to check back with her in about two weeks. This worked out fine as I was on my way to Zanzibar for a week in order to report on the African Film Festival.

I took a taxi back to the dusty dilapidated bus station where I purchased my ticket back to Dar Es Salaam. As the bus left the only paved highway in Tanzania, I looked at the shadow of Kilimanjaro and once again thought to myself how surreal all this seemed. I looked out of the window and gazed at the small huts that lined the road from Arusha to Dar, and wondered what it must be like to live life in such a localized way. I wondered what went through the people's minds as they labored close to the earth. Every day must seem like living on the edge, where there appeared to be a lack of abundance materially, yet they were bonded by such a deep social support.

I observed both how different our lives were and yet how similar. It is amazing how the human experience on so many different levels is fundamental to all cultures and transcends time and physicality. As I watched the children playing innocently and happily totally oblivious of the extreme poverty surrounding them, memories of my own childhood entered my mind. I thought back to how simple life seemed at that stage of our lives. The state of innocence is truly a powerful shield against the harsh realities of growing up in a developing world. It's ironic how we as humans are constantly vacillating between the longing for safety and security and the deep need for freedom. As I sat on this bus during my nine-hour drive, I thought about how many people here in Tanzania would give their right arm to live or at least visit the United States, the very place where I was seeking emotional distance and freedom of perspective from. It is an innate, universal human drive to find security, stability, and some semblance of a better life. Many of the people that I had spoken with stated that living in the US would afford them more freedom in their personal lives. The great irony of it is that I'd left the United States to come to Africa in order to find the same sense of freedom. However, my search had a more psychological and spiritual leaning as opposed to an economic or political reason behind it. Nevertheless, the same drive to escape from that which seems binding, the same restlessness that fuels the desire to go through insurmountable odds to reach it was the same. As I looked out of the window, I realized that all journeys no matter how large or small begin and end within ourselves.

Without realizing it, I drifted off into a deep sleep and awoke in the morning to a bright sun and the rustic sound of the vendors hovered around the huge bus terminal of Dar Es Salaam, which resembled a marketplace more than a bus terminal. The atmosphere in Dar was in stark contrast to that of Arusha. Getting off the bus, I was immediately overwhelmed by the intense humidity! Although a relatively small city by US standards, it is truly the melting pot of Tanzania. Luckily, my first impression of Dar Es Salaam wasn't by way of the bus terminal, with its random chaos and disorienting infrastructure, which would surely have been a major turnoff to any rationally thinking Westerner.

As I grabbed my luggage, I immediately saw the taxi driver who had taken me to the station for my trip to Arusha. He waved at me with a large smile. I quickly waved back and began approaching his taxi, only to be intercepted by three other drivers desperate to gain a client. One of the drivers was a white-haired gentleman with a grayish beard, a white Muslim *kufee* hat, and a very serious expression. He started yelling in rapid Swahili trying to convince both my original taxi driver and myself. I gave him a faint smile and with my broken Swahili said, "I already have a driver!" If looks could kill, then both the driver and I would be dead. As I entered my original taxi driver's car, the other drivers suddenly became quickly disinterested, as the reality that they weren't going to make any money became apparent.

The taxi driver seemed much more open and engaging than on our previous meeting. He stated that his name was Leonard and he was from a small town called Morogoro, located about 150 Km east of Dar Es Salaam. I asked him what he did before he drove a taxi. He told me that he worked in the tourist industry up north in Arusha. He stated that it was really the high point of his working career. He would get to meet people from different parts of the world such as Italy, Germany, Japan, etc. Before I had the chance to ask him why he stopped working in that industry, he stated, "I lost my job due to the privatization process here."

This is one of the many ironies of capitalism or rather privatization as it applies to industries in East Africa. Leonard went on to tell me, "I have five children all one year apart. I drive a taxi in order to feed my family. Sometimes I worked twelve hours or more just to make ends meet and keep food on the table." He supplemented his income by having a small garden in which he grew most of his family's food. This was an excellent example of the often-tedious living conditions that families face in Sub-Saharan Africa. One can live on the brink's edge, yet still finds the solidarity and comforts of loving relationships.

We drove with the windows down in Leonard's cab for two reasons; one was that he couldn't afford to get his air conditioning working and the other was that he needed to save gas. Unlike my long journeys in the hills of northern Tanzania, where the weather was cooler, the mystical mountains seemed to tease with both their majesty, and unattainably, here I could smell, see, and in some strange way feel the presence of the ocean. She at once encapsulated and defined this humid port city of Dar Es Salaam. If the sea is often described for its nurturing element and its ability to sustain life, then Dar was certainly the mother city of Tanzania.

Chapter Three

The Spice Island

"Hurry up and die, then you will speak as ancestors."
—Keteb Yacine

My new destination was Zanzibar, also known as the spice island. Its Arabic meaning is Zinj el-barr or Land of the Blacks. Zanzibar is an island wrapped in mysticism which lies about 50 miles east of the mainland of Tanzania. It has a very torrid history and a difficult relationship with the rest of Tanzania. For years, this island was the center of one of the largest slave trades between the Islamic Middle East and black Africa. At the turn of the century, Zanzibar became a British protectorate ruled under the guidance of Omani (Arab) sultans. This lasted until December of 1963 when Zanzibar gained its independence, which was then followed by a bloody revolution in which the blacks, led by the Afro-Shirazi political party, overthrew the ruling Arab sultans. To this day, there is a great disparity between Zanzibar's black African citizens and its Arab ones. This division existed in the extreme until the Zanzibar revolution of 1963. This revolution coupled with Zanzibar's marriage to with mainland Tanganyika led to the social, political, and economic empowerment of many black African Zanibarians.

As I waited in line for the ferry to pass, I was overwhelmed with the total change of atmosphere. There was something faintly Middle Eastern about the atmosphere as I was boarding the ferry. It was very crowded with everyone from British college students to Omani businessman. As the ferry pulled out to sea, my imagination became almost transverse in time. I felt that I was on an ancient journey sailing the winds of the peaceful Indian Ocean, looking for hidden treasures and valuables unknown. It was almost reminiscent of one of the older Sinbad adventure movies.

As I entered the ferry, there seemed to be a mad rush by all of the passengers to get a seat. I didn't understand why until the ship was underway.

Unlike the public transportation in the West, here the captain's primary concern was filling up the ferry to garnish the greatest amount of money. Safety and comfort were a mere afterthought. This seemed to be systemic throughout Tanzania. Even the Dala Dala minibusses race throughout the major cities with little regard for the safety of the passengers, other drivers, or pedestrians on the road. At the end the day, the primary objective was making a profit, regardless of what it took to get it.

As the ferry began its voyage toward Zanzibar, I gazed out at the horizon and looked at the skyline of Dar Es Salaam slowly receding away, and I thought to myself what an enchantingly beautiful city. Nevertheless, my mind was preoccupied with what lay ahead in Zanzibar. As the ferry moved along the calm, clear blue waters of the Indian Ocean, an older man with a slight build, long flowing gray beard, and an all-white outfit began to sing in what sounded like a mixture of Arabic and Swahili. He also had a very strange looking instrument that I would later find out was called an Oud. The music was beautiful and mesmerizing, with an almost hypnotic rhythm. Looking into the eyes of the musician, I could sense a deep serenity and calmness which seemed to pervade his very essence. His music helped add to an atmosphere that was already induced with mystery and a vague Asian feeling. Despite the intense heat and overcrowding, the people seemed to be very relaxed, almost content in their acceptance of the conditions in which we had to travel in. I sat next to two white (I assumed British citizens by their accents) travelers who looked thoroughly tired and worn out. They sat there drenched in sweat; the only white passengers on the ferry. Theirs were looks of resignation as if this wasn't their first experience in black Africa. Due to the lack of engine power of the ferry, what should have taken less than 50 minutes took up to an hour and a half. Once again this is part of the culture of many Sub-Saharan African countries. Many times in Africa, I was reminded of my early military experience in which we were often told to hurry up and wait, hurry up and wait. Being in the military in the USA is an entirely different reality than what one encounters in the day-to-day culture of the larger society.

It's very strange how certain manifestations can make one think of a completely unrelated event in one's life, often showing how most things are interconnected on one level or another. Here, I was thousands of miles away and yet still interconnecting certain happenings that on the surface seemed to be totally unrelated. It's amazing what similarities one can find when one travels to foreign places and yet still retain the same unconscious level of awareness, and the same subconscious level of awareness. This also permeates into the realm of culture. Once again, culture becomes such a defining mechanism that is in itself often transcendent.

As the ferry pulled into the Port of Stone Town, the intense rush of people who greeted the ship overtook me; it was utter chaos even by

African standards. Unlike the other two cities of Dar el Salaam and Arusha, I had no contacts here and no one to meet me at the bus terminal or airport. There was a stereotype in East Africa that Zanzibarian Kiswahili is the purest and most elegant form of speaking. I was a little intimidated by this because I knew that my mastery of Swahili left something to be desired.

Within minutes of getting off the ferry, I was bombarded with available taxis all offering to take me to the cheapest, best quality hotels. I looked around and saw a rather laid back young driver that had a somewhat clean cut look. I signaled him to come over and quickly entered his so-called cab. He asked me which hotel I was looking for, and I quickly responded that I was interested in the St. Monica's Hostel. I had no idea of where this hostel was located; I had actually received all of my information from a book. I tried to appear confident and sure as I didn't want him to have any inclination that I was completely at a loss regarding the island. As we drove off into the mysterious sunset of Zanzibar, the driver introduced himself as Ahmed. He stated that he was originally from the nearby island of Pemba, often considered the underdeveloped, mystical, smaller sister island of Zanzibar.

I asked him what brought him to Zanzibar, and Ahmed explained that there were virtually no jobs in Pemba and that to support himself he'd had to move to Zanzibar. He gave me a faint smile and then asked me why I had come to visit Zanzibar. Ahmed said that he was very surprised to see a Black American, as the majority of American visitors here were white. I told him that I was in Tanzania for work and that I had always wanted to visit Zanzibar. I said that it had a very exotic reputation in the west and was known as the Spice Island in many circles. He laughed and stated that there are definitely rich varieties of spices on the island. As we drove into the unexplored night, I thought to myself that Ahmed was undoubtedly a street tout, known in Swahili as a *papasi*. They are basically unregistered taxi drivers and guides. I did not intend to ask him for any official registration, and as long as we had a good chemistry between us, then I was okay with whatever legal papers he had or didn't have. There was a warmness that I felt from Ahmed, an openness that he gave off. As I have learned while living in Africa, it's always better to follow your gut reaction as opposed to relying on cold hard logic. This type of decision making would probably spell outright disaster in the West, but Africa truly defies logic!

Stone Town was like a dynamic museum of living history. Its architecture was a strange mixture of African, Arabic, and even Indian influences. One of the most distinguishing marks of Zanzibar architecture is its carved wooden doors. In ancient times, these doors served as symbols of wealth and social status. As we drove through the streets of Zanzibar, one would see these intricately designed doors in different homes throughout the town. I commented on the doors and Ahmed elaborated that many of the doors actually have carvings of passages from the Koran. He stated that other commonly seen symbols include the hand of Fatima, (representing spiritual protection), a fish (a symbol of fertility), and the lotus, (representing regeneration and spiritual transformation).

I ask Ahmed where he learned English so well. He told me that he learned basic English in school, but since he only attended school until the 6th grade, he continued to learn English on his own. Ahmed stated that so many English-speaking tourists come through Zanzibar that he had ample time to practice his skills! As we slowly pulled up to a small, narrow stone road leading to a hotel entrance, Ahmed stated that this was the

St. Monica's Hostel. Ahmed and I locked the door and entered the hotel together. There were three other people in line at the front desk, two ladies, and one man. They all seemed to be of European extraction. However, I wasn't able to pinpoint their specific accents. They were all tall and the man had what appeared to be a poor version of dreadlocks. I overheard the young man at the counter tell them that all of the rooms were booked for the evening. I had Ahmed ask the young man working behind the counter if there were any rooms available. Being that we were both black, and Ahmed was doing the talking, maybe he would make an exception. However, the young man gave a very polite no, which I believed was sincere.

He then suggested that we go to a nearby hotel named the Flamingo Guest House. We pulled into the lobby and saw a very attractive looking Arab girl working at the desk. She was wearing the traditional black Islamic headdress. She spoke with a very soft voice, and her demeanor was demure if not self-effacing. She told us that there were a couple of rooms of double bedrooms available for the night. Ahmed told her that I only needed a single room. However, she insisted very politely that the only rooms available were doubles. Ahmed took me to the side and stated that most hotels say that to foreigners to charge a higher rate. I was exhausted, slightly frustrated, and certainly in no mood to negotiate; or worse, look for another hotel.

Ahmed helped me with my luggage upstairs, and we parted with the verbal agreement of meeting in the morning so that he could take me on a tour through the island. The room was surprisingly spacious with two small beds covered with the traditional mosquito nets, which were prevalent throughout Tanzania. The room was painted blue and white and was decorated with *dhows* which are the traditional sail boats that have been utilized in Zanzibar since the early days of trading.

As tired as I was that evening, I was unable to sleep. I can recall turning and tossing throughout the night. My mind seemed to be running at a hundred miles an hour, thinking of everything from the possibility of failing at my project to which city back home would be more conducive to live in. As I began to doze off, I could hear the busy chatter pick up downstairs. I wasn't sure if I was dreaming since I was in the limbo state of being half awake and half asleep. When I finally fell asleep, the phone rang, waking me. Reception downstairs told me that a man was waiting for me. I assumed that it was the taxi driver. I told them to tell Ahmed that I would be downstairs in twenty minutes.

I quickly jumped in the shower, fumbled through my luggage, and threw on my shorts and a T-shirt. I was rushing downstairs when the maid insisted that I sit for a minute and get the free breakfast that was part of the accommodations. I decided that anything geared towards helping me to save money was positive. I decided to grab a quick bite to eat and avoid buying breakfast on the street. I sat down in a small middle room that was between the second floor TV room and the hotel restroom. As I sat there trying to eat my free breakfast quickly, I was approached by a rather tall, somewhat goofy-looking blonde with an American accent. She asked me a question in Kiswahili to which I responded that I didn't speak Kiswahili. I then asked her where she was from in the States. She said that she was from California. I told her that I was originally from New Jersey. She gave a loud laugh and said that I looked like a guy she knew from Zanzibar, and that was why she had addressed me in Kiswahili.

She introduced herself and stated that she worked for a US-sponsored refugee program based in Nairobi, Kenya. I told her that I had my own company that sold used medical supplies and equipment. She asked me if I had ever considered working with refugees. She stressed that as an African American, there was a great need. Although White, Karen Joseph, stated: "African refugees would appreciate and be able to relate more to a person of African descent." I told her that I had some experience teaching English as a second language to refugees in the United States and that I would consider it. I realized that this could be a great way for me to supplement my income, learn more about the health needs of the diverse countries in Africa, and make a difference!

I asked Karen how long she was staying. "I am leaving this evening," she said. I told her that was too bad because I had just arrived. Looking down at my watch, I realized that I was late, and my taxi driver was waiting for me downstairs. She told me that we could ride together in the taxi and that she could show me the town. I told her that it sounded like a great idea, and I would meet her downstairs.

I greeted Ahmed with the typical *habari gani*, Kiswahili for hello, and he greeted me back with the words *inzori sana*. I apologized for being late, and he gave me a large smile and told me not to worry about it, that we were now on Zanzibar time! I laughed and said that we have a similar expression in the United States called colored-folk time! He was a little confused about the expression so I went on to explain that colored was a name often used to refer to black Americans, especially during the earlier portion of this century. I looked up the old wooden stairwell, and I saw Karen Joseph coming down with a large load of luggage. Ahmed and I jumped up and helped her with her luggage, which at the time seemed like the only polite thing to do. I introduced Karen Joseph to my driver Ahmed. They greeted each other very cautiously. We put Karen Joseph's luggage into the taxi and then she began to take charge. She asked me what I was interested in seeing. I told her that I was interested in seeing some of the historical sights. She then asked Ahmed if he was familiar with the section of Stone Town, and he gave her a very wide grin and quietly responded, in his thickly accented English, of course!

It was then mid-morning, and I was starting to grasp the vastness and complexity of culture on the island. Driving through the streets of Zanzibar is truly like being transported back in time. The cobbled stone streets were full of small bazaars, small shops, that specialized in selling local arts and crafts. The wonderful aroma of assorted spices mixed with the sultry sound of the *Taarab*, Zanzibar's famous export music that combines African, Indian, and Arabic influences. All these elements combined to create a truly mysterious, ancient, and almost surreal atmosphere.

For the next five minutes, Karen Joseph went on and on about what she liked and disliked in Zanzibar. If I didn't know any better, I would have assumed that she was native to the island or at least had lived there for a substantial amount of time. She then directed the driver to go to the site called the House of Wonders. She said, "this will be a fascinating place to visit since it is sort of in the middle of everything. You may also be interested in attending the International Film Festival held this week."

I gave a rather enthusiastic response. "I am a huge fan of foreign films, especially those with an emphasis on African stories and culture! I can't believe my luck; I honestly had no idea that there was a film festival taking place during my visit to Zanzibar." Both Ahmed and Karen started giggling, obviously somewhat amused with my intense enthusiasm. Our first stop was going to be at *Beit El Ajab,* "house of wonders" in English. This was a historically significant building, according to Ahmed, with a vast amount of information about the early history of Zanzibar. Having been a history buff all of my life, I couldn't wait to enter. The House of Wonders is one of the largest structures in Zanzibar. It was originally created as a ceremonial palace. Its primary theme is the *dhow* which stands as the intricate symbol of everything Swahili. On first entering the building, I was almost overwhelmed by the giant-sized dhow also known as an *mtepe* or the traditional Swahili carved sailing ship built without any modern tools; the wood held together simply by coconut fibers and natural pegs.

Our next stop was the Beit El-Sahel, or Palace Museum, a place dedicated to the history of the old rulers of Zanzibar. I was very surprised at how much of Zanzibar's history was intertwined not only with Europe and the Middle East but also America! There was a lot of focus on the elaborate marriages of princes from Zanzibar with royalty from Europe, the sultans amassing of great levels wealth and affluence, and the vast numbers of wives that each of these historical figures had. As the museum guide spoke, there was a very real feeling that everyone's mind was somewhere else. All I could think about at this point was the International Film Festival. As my mind wondered, my attention was immediately brought back to the present when our guide mentioned the old slave market!

We went outside to the Anglican cathedral which we were told was next to the old slave market. I could clearly see some discomfort on the face of Karen who seemed a bit disinterested. I went on to have a side conversation with Ahmed about the impact of slavery on the island of Zanzibar. He told me that thousands of slaves were taken from the interior of Africa and shipped here and also numerous other destinations throughout the Middle

East. Karen Joseph was quick to point out that Arabs and traders of Islam carried out this slavery. I simply nodded in agreement, thinking in the back of my mind that Europe and Christianity had also played a very large part in slavery in our part of the world.

The actual slave market didn't have any existing tangible monuments outside of a couple of small abandoned old holding cells next to a hostel. The grounded metaphors were very symbolic for me, and I was thrilled to be able to visit and pay homage to those ancestors who suffered such an ugly destiny. My mind wondered back in time as I thought of the Nigerian priest in New York who said that my guardian spirit was Oya, goddess of change and transformation. What other type of change is as great as the transition of death? As we wandered around the courtyard, Karen reminded us of the film festival. She asked, "Ahmed, what time do you have?" "Three p.m.," he answered.

"We've got to hurry then because I have to catch the ferry back to the mainland Tanzania, and I want to stop by the Zanzibar International Film Festival." I was thrilled as this was one of my primary reasons for coming to Zanzibar.

I ask, "Ahmed, how are you feeling?" I wanted to know how much time or rather money was accumulating during this great sightseeing tour. He softly grabbed my hand and with his normally soft-spoken tone said, "please don't worry about it. We can work something out later." As the three of us approached the Zanzibar Cultural Centre, my attention was immediately focused on the girl at the reception. She was breathtakingly beautiful. Standing about 5'7" with a near-perfect athletic build, she had stunning, sparkling jet black eyes and clear, smooth almost golden skin. As Karen Joseph approached the ticket box to find out information about movie times and prices, I was instantly overwhelmed with the beauty of the attendant's smile. For an instant, I actually thought that this could be love at first sight. What I would come to realize is that this would be one of many infatuations with the beautiful if somewhat elusive women of Mother Africa.

I figured out that I would wait until Karen was going to leave before I would make my approach. She and I agreed that we had to go to a bank to change money. We asked Ahmed if he could take us to the nearest bank and once again we were in the cab and on our way down a cobbled stone street, transported into what seemed to be a voyage back in time. We arrived at a small bureau change department in a local NBC bank. I went to the ATM to withdraw some money, but Karen had to wait in line to speak with a teller since she needed to exchange money. I decided to wait in the small waiting area which was located to the left of this all-white building. As I waited there, I noticed an Arab lady dressed in the traditional black *hijab* from the neck down. What was unusual was that her face wasn't covered. As always in traditional Muslim societies, I was very wary of looking or speaking to strange women, especially if they seemed conservative in anyway. As I tried my best to avoid any direct eye contact with her, I heard, "hello, how are you?" I looked around and thought that it was coming from someone behind me. Once again I heard, "excuse me, how are you doing?"

This time, I recognized the accent to be American! As I turned to the left, I noticed that the Arab lady was speaking to me. I was totally bewildered. I turned to her and responded back with a very apprehensive hello of my own. After a few minutes, she asked me if I was an American. I shook my head and asked if she could tell from my accent. She simply smiled and stated that she was also originally from the States. She extended her hand. "My name is Rahima." She said that she was originally from St. Louis, Missouri, but had been living in Zanzibar for the last five years. I told her that my name was Hassan and that I was originally from New Jersey. We both sat back and burst out laughing. I told her that I was very shocked when she spoke to me because I just assumed that she was an Arab from Zanzibar. I then went on to say that I didn't know that she were a sister from back home.

I noticed from the far corner of my eye that Karen Joseph was looking somewhat bewildered at the close and seemingly intimate conversation that I was having with this Arab lady. As Karen approached, she was very enthusiastic and open; she extended her hand out and introduced herself to Rahima. She was somewhat reticent on her part, seemingly much more aloof in her greetings with Karen than myself. I spoke. "Karen, Rahima is also from the States like us."

Karen's initial warm openness changed. It was very subtle, but noticeable to me. I was somewhat bewildered at the time but left it at that. As we got ready to go, Rahima and I exchanged contact information, and she kindly invited me to her home. She was also very interested in my medical journalism and suggested that we may be able to do joint projects together in Zanzibar. Initially, this sounded like a dream come true. However, I was starting to realize it's better to wait and let things manifest before making any concrete plans. We quickly exchanged contact information before I set out in the taxi again. We headed towards the ferry that would take Karen back to Dar Es Salaam. On the way there all I could seem to think about was meeting the beautiful lady that was posted at the ticket booth at the film festival. Pulling up to the ferry station was outright chaos. As I had originally arrived at night, I'd been able to bypass to a certain degree this intense level of activity. As we dropped Karen off, I thanked her for taking the time to show me around the island. We exchanged contact information, and I told her that I was interested in following up on the possible job opportunity working with refugees. We said our goodbyes and Ahmed and I were soon off into the sunset, heading back towards the waterfront close to the International Film Festival.

As we traveled back through the dark, narrow cobblestone streets of Stone Town observing and at the same time feeling the spiritual richness of the town, I decided to put the window down to ingest the essence of the island. The aromas of frankincense, exotic spices, and fish engulfed me. With all of the activity going on outside, my mind still raced with thoughts of the beautiful woman that was in the ticket booth. I wondered what her name was? Her origin? Was she part of the film festival? Maybe she was a filmmaker herself? All of these questions raced through my head as we drove within these mysterious streets.

As we approached the old fort which housed the International Film Festival, I could feel my heart beating faster. It was reminiscent of the feeling I would get when I approached a girl that I had a crush on in high school, apprehensive and somewhat craven. After taking a deep breath, I asked Ahmed if he could drop me off and pick me up around 10 p.m. He told me that he would be unable to do so because of a prior commitment that he had with his family. However, he told me that he had a reliable friend that would surely be there to pick me up on time. We agreed and parted ways. I headed straight for the ticket booth, hoping to find the beautiful young lady that had been there over two hours ago. As I approached the booth, I only saw a lady that was wearing the traditional

Islamic outfit and was covered from head to toe. I looked around in utter impatience. Here, I was finally free to approach whom I wanted, and the person that I desired to speak to had disappeared as quickly as she had appeared. Then I began to wonder if this beautiful and mysterious person was a figment of my imagination. As I approached the ticket counter, I asked the young lady what time the next film was playing. However, in my mind, I wanted so desperately to inquire about the whereabouts of the beautiful young lady that was working at the booth earlier. Being as it may, I decided that fate wasn't on my side and decided to focus simply on enjoying the film festival.

I was informed that the movie didn't play for another hour and a half. Since I had time to burn, I decided to explore the area. As the sun was setting and the weather was absolutely gorgeous, I decided to take a walk through the famous Darajani market, which was close by. As I approached the market, the smell of salt water became overwhelming. I tried to climb my way through the cluster of street vendors selling everything from handcrafted goods to fruits, fish, and vegetables. I then noticed a large number of foreigners in the mix, with accents ranging from Cockney English, Afrikaans, French, Arabic, and German. A vibrant energy pulsated from the market. Extremely hungry at this point, I figured that this would be a good time to indulge in some authentic traditional Zanzibar cuisine. I looked at several of the venders, and although the smell was somewhat enticing to an empty stomach, raw fish, heat, and sellers not wearing any gloves just didn't seem like a good idea.

Near a small beachfront bar, I overheard two people speaking with distinctly American accents. Feeling a little home sick, I decided to introduce myself. For these parts, they were an unusually attractive

Anglo-American couple. She was tall, with brownish blond hair, unblemished skin, straight white teeth and piercing sky blue eyes. The man was also very tall with sharp, almost flawless chiseled features, and a full head of grayish blond hair, with a very pedigreed "old money" aura. I first asked them which part of the States they came from. The woman answered that they were employees of World Bank here on business. I then introduced myself and told them that I was from the Philadelphia area here working as a journalist. The lady proceeded to ask me more about my job. She wanted to know what type of journalism I was involved in. As a young and upcoming journalist, I was easily flattered into conversing about my future plans and vision to write for an international NGO in Africa. At the middle of my conversation, I noticed that it was primarily a one-way conversation. There was a lot of information coming from me, but very little being exchanged back from them.

I suddenly turned the tables and asked which organization they worked for. There was a clear uncomfortable reticence that was given off by both of them as I began to pry into their trip here to Zanzibar Island. The man stated that they both worked for the World Bank in Washington D.C. He said this with very little eye contact, and I really began to get the impression that they were both hiding something. My first instinct was that they were American intelligence officers monitoring Islamic fundamentalist groups here in Zanzibar. This would make sense at a time when tensions were so high between the United States and many Islamic countries.

Back home in the States, there would be a trial involving a prominent government member involved with exposing an undercover intelligence agent named Valerie Plame. I can't be one hundred percent sure, but to this day, I feel strongly that the mysterious American lady with the regal bearing was her.

I excused myself from these fellow Americans and headed south, following the beach and listening to the vivid sounds of the sea as it sang its smooth melodious song of centuries-old stories of pirates, sailors, adventurers, visionaries, thieves, princess, and whores. Walking through the local market I wondered if I would ever see the beautiful woman who had been working at the ticket booth. Maybe it was just a passing phantom, a dream, or a lost story in my head.

I walked further down the beach until I came to a restaurant named the Monsoon Café. It caught my eye with its Eastern and somewhat mystical design. As I entered the restaurant, I was even more impressed with the overall ambiance and aura of the place. It reminded me of a small café located in the middle of a Caribbean island. As I entered the front door, a tall handsome Swahili-looking gentleman greeted me. He greeted me in the gentle *habari*, which is a basic Swahili greeting used very casually throughout East Africa. A distinct-looking tall gentleman with smooth caramel-colored skin, he was polite, but there was a reticence and distance in his demeanor that was unmistakable. He quickly seated me, gave me a menu, and gently seemed to vanish into the exoticism of the restaurant. Once again I was transported in time to the impeccably decorated atmosphere that played traditional-style music such as *taarab* and other indigenous sounds. There was the option of sitting on the traditional-style Swahili floor cushions versus the more modern Western-style chairs.

As I waited for the meal to be served, my eyes were fixated on a beautiful young lady that was sitting off in the far north corner of the restaurant. I wasn't a hundred percent sure, but as I focused my eyes more,

I thought that this lady bore a strange resemblance to the young lady that I'd seen hours before at the film festival. I pretended to get up and go to the restroom just to get a better look at her. As I walked by her the first time, my heart was racing so fast it felt as if it was going to jump a hole in my chest. I was so distracted that I walked into the ladies room by accident. After quickly realizing my mistake, I rushed out and ran into the men's room in utter embarrassment. Luckily, no one was around. I washed my face and looked in the mirror and semi-practiced what I was going to say to her if this was the same young lady that I was seemingly so infatuated with.

As I went back into the dining area, I mustered up enough courage to ask her if she worked at the International Film Festival. She smiled at me and said that she only volunteered there. She asked me if I was going to attend, and I told her that I bought tickets for the last showing at 9 p.m. I then asked her if I could pull up a seat next to her. With the typical Tanzanian hospitality, she graciously said of course. As I sat down next to her, her intense dark eyes and beautiful smile once again bewitched me. She spoke perfect English with a slightly British accent.

I asked, "where are your origins? Where are you from?"

"My mother is half-German and half-Tanzanian. I am a full-time student at the University of London and am only here in Zanzibar to volunteer for the film festival. Now your turn, where are you from?"

"The US."

She gave me a surprised look and asked what I was doing so far from home.

I told her that I was a journalist seeking to cover stories on NGO's working with health care issues in East Africa. I explained to her that I had started a small used medical supply company that was looking to gain a presence in Eastern Africa. She agreed with me. "There is a very urgent need to improve the health care infrastructure in Zanzibar." I then went on to explain to her that this was more than just a work project for me, but a deep-seated passion that burned in my heart.

I wanted to change the conversation back to her, so I decided to ask her whether or not she preferred living in London to Zanzibar.

"Well, both places have their good points and bad ones. In terms of weather and hospitality, Zanzibar wins hands down. However, when it comes to infrastructure and everyday things working in a somewhat orderly and predictable fashion, I prefer London."

I then interjected that for food, both selection and taste, Zanzibar wins hands down. We each burst out laughing, as she strongly agreed. I went on to ask her if she had ever visited the United States and she said no, but then quickly interjected that her boyfriend's parents lived in Canada. She stated that they were hopefully going to visit them next year in Montreal, and hopefully they would be able to cross the USA border. I was totally crushed regarding the news of a boyfriend. However, I did an excellent job of hiding my feelings and actually appearing to be happy to hear the news. I went on to ask her if her boyfriend was Canadian and she told me that he was Italian, but his parents lived in Canada. As I began to listen between the lines of what she was really saying or rather not saying, I could perceive a sense of elitism and slight snobbery. I would later find out that this attitude was incredibly pervasive amongst the mixed race class in Africa, as well as other non-black Africans.

As the conversation progressed, I became bored. I kept looking at my watch to ensure that I didn't' miss the opening movie at the film festival. It's ironic how something can look so inviting, but beyond the surface, there is a myriad of complex interactions that give one an entirely different perception. This has been my experience in Africa thus far. Most things are not as they appear, shadows at every corner, mirages in a vast desert, enticing one to come closer only to find an illusion. At every step of the journey, I thought that I would find one thing only to discover something entirely different. I thought that I was seeking a particular path only to be redirected in another direction. That was the flow of my journey in Africa, my exploration without and within.

The sun began to set like a long beautiful dance troupe with its multi-colored display of burnt orange and purple. The cool breeze whispered untold secrets. To this day, I believe that Zanzibar has the most beautiful sunsets in the world!

The featured filmed was about a child that was AIDS victim in the Congo. The filmmaker was a British journalist who seemed to have extensive experience writing and working in Africa. The film was made in Zambia and featured the life of a Zambian teacher who was struck with AIDS. It was a very realistic and stark look at the impact of HIV/AIDS on the African families in this part of the world. I thought that the movie did a splendid job at covering the emotional, financial, and social issues and taboos that come along with one having the disease in this part of the world. There was very reserved applause after the movie that is so typical of East African culture. I was probably one of the loudest in my clapping. I must admit that I was very impressed with the subject matter, if not the overall direction of the movie. Again, this opinion is very subjective as I have a strong penchant for documentaries, especially foreign ones.

It was a wonderful way to end a very satisfying and exotic adventure. It was time for me to head back to the mainland of Tanzania and begin pursuing serious work and/or interview leads. I had to prepare myself now for the slow journey back to Dar Es Salam. Sailing back, I thought about the beautiful language of Swahili and the hybrid culture that it has created here. Wherever Swahili is spoken as the predominant language, it has created a mélange and blending of cultures, primarily Arab and Bantu, but with undeniable assortments of various other races and creeds which is infused by the residence of the lands and touched by the winds of the western Indian Ocean. It is the unique gift of being able to assimilate cultures, histories, and even genes, without interfering with its essential core identity that gives continuity and vibrancy to Zanzibar's nationality. The culture here is unshaken by the multiplicity of races and ethnicities.

The Doors of No Return, Elmina Slave Castle, Ghana

Traditional Nubian home: Aswan, Egypt

Colonial monument: Morogoro, Tanzania

Ancient Ruins: Zanzibar Island

United Nations Center: Arusha, Tanzania

Watch Tower: Robben Island Prison

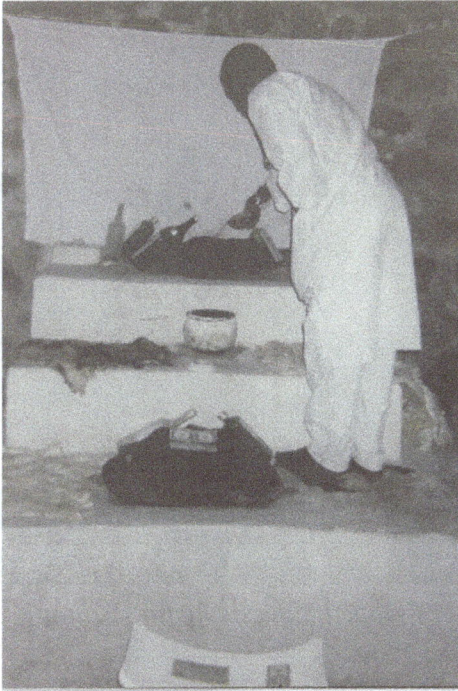

Traditional AKAN Priest,
Cape Coast Ghana

Lake Victoria, UGANDA

Escaped Slaves, Darfur, Sudan

Afro-Brazilian Santeria Practitioner, Brooklyn, New York

Tea Plantation, Kenya

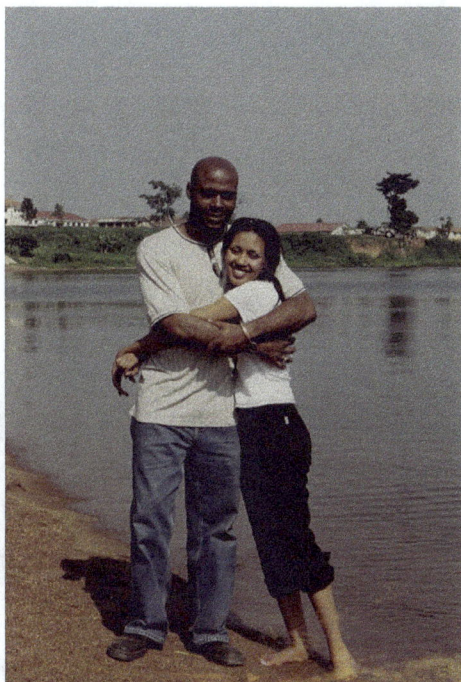

Fazia and author Jinja Uganda

Female Slave Dungeon, Elmina Slave Castle, Ghana

Nelson Mandela's Prison Cell: Robben Island, South Africa

*Watch Tower Kakuma Refugee
Camp, Northern Kenya*

Sunset: Stone Town, Zanzibar

Chapter Four

Little London In Africa

"In Africa, the first thing you learn is to live life as it comes."
—Paul Morand

There is an old saying in East Africa, "If you want to know the end of something, look at its beginning." My very first experience in Kenya was a disaster. The evening that I arrived, I checked into a hotel in downtown Nairobi named The Three Sixty-Nine. During the ride, there was a British expatriate that apprised me that the hotel rates were cheaper during the week. However, I had to ask because the marked up rate was never changed on the billboard by the front desk. As I left the minibus and entered the streets of downtown Nairobi, I was transplanted to a different world.

Unlike Tanzania, which was actually the poorer of the two countries, Nairobi had a pervasive darkness that seemed to permeate the air. There was uneasiness in the faces of its citizens; a look of deep dissatisfaction and utter distrust. There was a hunger in the eyes of the homeless children that I observed on the streets of Nairobi. As my later experiences would reveal, my first instincts about the Kenyan culture were right, at least as it related to my experiences and me. To this day, Kenya remains one of my least favorite of African nations. It's ironic. The early Tanzanian president,

Julius Nyerere stated that if any African wanted to travel to London, all they had to do was visit Kenya! I found this to be very true. Of course a true cosmopolitan atmosphere as well as the sense of internationalism was lacking, however, there was more of a sense of knowingness and confidence from the people in comparison with next-door neighbor Tanzania. I had a scheduled interview with the US refugee resettlement agency. I took a taxi from the hotel to an area called Kilieshwa in Nairobi.

This was a somewhat upscale area of the city full of expatriates and professional middle class Kenyans. Even there, I felt an overwhelming sense of uneasiness, wariness, and a sense of being watched. Maybe it was the subtle sense of mistrust that seemed so pervasive throughout Kenyan culture. I rode in what seemed to be a large British taxi from the '20s. They were in stark contrast to the small Japanese models used in Tanzania. There was also this overwhelming sense that I had been transplanted back to a British colony in the 1930s. I don't know if it was the infrastructure of the country or the overall atmosphere of it, but it left me feeling a longing for the somewhat progressive African atmosphere of Tanzania.

As I entered the large courtyard waiting to be interviewed, I was immediately overwhelmed by the strong sense of isolation that engulfed the huge numbers of refugees who were there waiting. Waiting because their life was on hold; hoping that there was a pot of gold at the end of the rainbow in the Western white countries that lay across the sea. I sat there and tried to place myself in their situation, tried to see the world from the eyes of someone who felt as if he/she belonged nowhere. Ironically, growing up as an Afro-American in the USA, I could sometimes identify with this feeling of isolation and misplacement. Living back home there was always a sense of not belonging, of being somewhat of an alien in my own country.

As silly as it sounded, I felt more connected to my countries of origin while in Africa than I ever had being there! I was immediately absorbed with the plight of the refugees. I almost identified with their sense of not belonging anywhere, but I never felt their perception of powerlessness.

It seemed like an eternity before someone came out to interview me. A young lady slowly opened the door and called my name in a very low and unsure manner. I walked up to the door and introduced myself. She seemed surprised and a little uncomfortable. She slowly opened the door to let me inside the old building, which looked more like a small county jail as opposed to a refugee-processing center.

Entering the office, I could feel that all eyes were on me. This was surely a warning of things to come in the future. One thing that Africa was teaching me was to trust my intuition; trust the inner voice in myself. As I would later find out, my first feelings about this organization and the people who worked here were certainly on point.

After waiting for over half an hour, I was approached by a stockily built man with receding blond hair and glasses. He extended his hand, and with a deeply Southern draw stated that his name was Scott. He apologized for the wait and said very frankly that he thought it was a different person by the name of Hassan who was coming to interview. We both slightly smiled with that familiar uncomfortable quirk that one has when they're really not sure of what to say or do.

Scott looked at my resume, smiled slightly, and then told me that in all honesty, I was probably a little over-qualified for the position. He went into more detail about the position, what would be required of me, and what the expectations were. He stated that I would start out as a resettlement officer, which simply consisted of going into refugee camps and writing the stories of potential refugees who would be coming to the USA. We would prepare the case files for INS agents who would make the final decision. As my first passion was health care in Africa, this seemed like an ideal experience. I would be able to work hand in hand with international NGOs. I would be able to learn about the infrastructure of many Sub-Saharan African nations first hand. This would possibly give me a gauge into writing realistic and compelling real stories about this part of the world.

We finished the interview off on a very positive note. He stated, "you're almost guaranteed of securing the job. However, the background checks as well as getting the official working papers through the Kenyan government could take well over three months." I decided that this would be an ideal time to go back to the States, regroup my things, and come back a little better prepared.

As I traveled back to my hotel, I decided to stop off and get a drink in the lounge. As I sat there rather satisfied with my expedited hiring process, I noticed a very attractive Somali girl staring at me. Feeling a little self-confident and self-satisfied, I approached her very openly and boldly, which normally isn't my style. I introduced myself as Hassan and told her that I was new there. She smiled and answered, "my name is Yasmina." I asked, "are you from Kenya?"

"No, I am a refugee originally from Somalia. Most of my family are dead or still stuck in Somalia. I am alone in Kenya without any support or income."

It was at this point that I realized she was a prostitute simply working in different hotels trying to make ends meet. As I would later find out, this was very common in Nairobi and most large cities in Kenya. The context of prostitution was a little different than in the West. In Kenya, prostitution was seen as a practical mechanism for survival in a world in which there are very little outlets for financial freedom or independence. There wasn't the great moral conflict that is often attached to it like in the West. In fact, I would even venture to say that the whole concept of romance is definitely a Johnny-come-lately in African culture. Historically, in many Sub-Saharan African cultures, there was the concept of marrying for the benefit of the clan or ethnic group. I have seen this acted out from the Nilotic Nubians of Upper Egypt to the Bantu peoples of southern Africa.

Again, one dangerous misconception that many Westerners often have, myself included, is trying to judge the moral aspects of African culture from our own standards. This can cause a myriad of misinterpretations and misunderstandings. Although many people would argue that this isn't an important principle to be argued; nevertheless, it has its being from the same root cause of most conflicts in the world.

I sat there in my hotel room and thought to myself how I would be able to live and work in such a place that was so different from not only my worldview but my expectations of what I thought Africa should be or even what it could be.

Of all the twelve African nations that I have visited, I found Kenya to bleed the most with the stench of old-world colonialism, to hold on the inferior mindset of old world Africa, and to most value the European ethos! It was in Kenya that I could honestly say that I had my most intimate relationship with Africa. It was in Kenya that I had my most trying relationship with Africa. It was also there that I felt the most challenged in embracing my African ancestry. The racist legacy here was subtly pernicious. Black people still show a vestigial diffidence when in the company of Asians or whites, the result of years of deteriorating of self-esteems over more than a hundred years of being at the bottom of the social ladder in their own country. Many still lack self-esteem. They feel that their skin isn't light enough, hair isn't soft enough, and their schools aren't good enough. Yet even in Kenya, Africa would show her paradoxical face. I was lucky enough to be introduced to David Kamau, a Kenyan journalist and writer whose uncle was part of the Kenyan rebellion against colonialism better known as Mau Mau. I was very grateful to have met him and wanted to know more about this historic event. David was a thin, thoughtful man in his mid-'60s. Tall, dark-skinned and with a large gap in his front teeth, he was self-assured and scholarly. David said, "Kenya was home to one of the most substantive and successful revolutionary movements in the history of the so-called developing world, The Mau Mau War."

Similar to the Maji Maji revolt in Tanzania, Mau Mau was a nationalist revolt against colonial oppression. In Kenya, this rebellion was aimed at the British Empire as opposed to the German colonial powers in neighboring Tanzania. The uprising was caused by both social-economic and political repression of the *Kikuyu* ethnic group, the largest in Kenya, at the hands of white British settlers and the colonial state. The exact origins of Mau Mau are uncertain at best, and ambiguous at worst. What is clear is that Kenya's largest ethnic group, the Kikuyu, were disgruntled over land disputes. Because of their size and influence, the Kikuyu were able to create serious social and political upheaval more than any other tribe. The organization known as Mau Mau connected themselves to each other through a process that became known as the Oath. This oath was a ceremonial pledge and commitment to the subversion of British colonialism. The movement was energized by the vision of local African mythos. Thousands took oaths, pledging their very lives to the cause of liberation. If they failed to do everything possible to help their revolution, they would die as a result of the oath, not by the bullet from the gun, but rather by supernatural means. The oathing ceremony transformed the way the Kikuyu saw their spiritual reality. Many turned their backs on Western religions such as Christianity and returned to their traditional ancestral religions.

In the beginning, most Mau Mau members joined because they had land grievances or were disgruntled because of the inequities within the colonial educational and political systems. The nationalist movement attempted to unite the Kikuyu, along with other black Kenyans in order to gain more direct political representation as well as land rights. The often violent nature of Mau Mau movement drew intense scrutiny and eventual military responses from the colonial government. The heavy-handed response from the British government forced many Mau Mau leaders to retreat into the forest of the hills. It was from these lonely and dark forests that the most successful attacks were organized against both British colonial structures and fellow Africans who were loyal to the British.

I asked, "why would their fellow Africans feel any sense of loyalty towards the British?"

"These Africans were known as Loyalists to both the British and the Mau Mau. There was a myriad of reasons for this misguided loyalty. Many would not take the oath because of their deeply held Christian beliefs. Others had something to gain either socially or economically with the British, and the vast majority were simply afraid of the unknown or change."

I smiled and quoted, "better the devil you know than the devil you don't know."

In the Shadows of the Ancestors

David told me that his great-uncle had served in Burma during the Second World War under the flag of the British. He returned home to Kenya to find that his family land had been confiscated under the so-called White Paper Act. This act recommended for sanitation purposes that Natives be kept as far as possible away from Nairobi's white and Asian populations. The colonial power had established in Kenya a system of institutionalized racism and discrimination against the indigenous population. It was estimated that half of the urban workers in private companies and one-third of those working in the public sector often received wages too low even to provide for their essential living needs. My uncle fit into this group. He had two wives and six children to feed."

I stood up rather anxiously and asked how people could be so barbaric. David leaned back, stretched out his arms, and with the calm wisdom of an elder said, "every group's reality and sense of fairness is different. The British's sense of reality was unique. A 1950 colonial report stated that the essential natural resource in Kenya is its land, and we consider it as a part of our colony. They considered it imperative for both the well-being of their empire, as well as the safety and development of the barbaric black natives, that the choicest land be developed and settled by white British settlers. In their minds, this was for the sake of progress and civilization. The underlying philosophy of the settlers was that Kenyan land was theirs by right of development and achievement. They seriously thought that both the black's land and worldview had disappeared forever. During the days of colonialism, they thought that Africans, such as my father, were just existing in a world created by Europeans, all issued under the vision of enlightenment and humanitarianism."

We stared at one another for a long time. I broke the silence by asking David if he considered the Mau Mau movement a mere rebellion or true revolution. He leaned close and smiled. "Young man, what were you told about the Mau Mau in the US?"

I replied, "in school, we were briefly taught that Mau Mau was a terrorist rebellion, led by the Kenya's dominant ethnic group, the Kikuyu. The Kikuyu extremists were furious about what they saw as the theft of their ancestral land by British settlers, so they launched a vicious killing spree from the jungle against all whites living in Kenya."

David retorted, "my friend, the Mau Mau movement was just as much a revolution as the American or French Revolutions. Although Mau Mau was technically not successful in the classic sense of overturning the British government, it forced the British to enter the door of granting Kenya its independence. They were much more disciplined and organized than the British government could ever have expected. Mau Mau had a rigid hierarchy of soldiers, leaders, and loyalty from the masses of Kikuyu and other Black Africans. Mau Mau were both the architects of social change and the victims of social upheaval. Therefore, Mau Mau's overall goal and vision to banish the colonial powers out of Kenya and gain a political voice certainly made this a revolution."

I told David that I could not thank him enough for giving me another insight into the history of Kenya. This allowed me to gain more perspective and to feel more sympathy for the culture and people here.

It would be less than a month before I would return to Nairobi from the States. During my short stay home, my mind, heart, and spirit were still in Africa. It seemed as if the majority of my time was spent on the Internet connecting with my newfound friends from East Africa. After two weeks,

I was notified that my working papers arrived in Nairobi and that I should report no later than a week from my notification. Well, this was both good and bad news.

The holidays were coming and my mother was going to be shattered when she found out that I wasn't going to be around for Christmas. My first thoughts were to push my arrival date back. I went on to call one of the officers named Marsha, whom I briefly interviewed with while back in Nairobi. After reaching her on the phone after several attempts to get through, I was very surprised at her original reception. Her tone was very condescending and slightly rude. I then restated whom I was hoping that she had a case of mistaken identity. Her rudeness and underlying belligerence seemed to increase. For the first time, I actually reconsidered taking the assignment. I asked myself what type of organization would hire such a person to work with their public relations division in this manner. I thought about it and quickly regained my perspective. This was a small unknown NGO working with refugees in Kenya. This wasn't a multi-media Fortune 500 company based in the middle of Manhattan dealing with high-end global clients. In retrospect, I realized how preposterous it was to rationalize such unprofessional behavior. It was there in Kenya that I learned that the outlandish often reconciles with the logical, and where the factual is married to the speculative, and the holy often unites with the profane.

I decided that it was futile to take any of this personally. I had to look at the long-term vision of what I wanted to achieve and certainly this job in East Africa was in alignment with my long-term goals. Before long I was on the plane again heading back to East Africa; this time Nairobi, Kenya. I was a little more confident about what to expect. My goals were clearer, my will more determined, and my vision extremely focused. Now my overall knowledge of East Africa was a little more experiential.

On the first day of my arrival in Nairobi, I contacted an old friend Richard from Tanzania. He told me that I could stay with a relative of his in a section of the town called Kileshwa. The next day, two aged Indian men picked me up at my hotel, both being much older than I expected. The first man greeted me in what oddly seemed to be broken English with a very strong Swahili accent. The next gentleman spoke with a pristine, clear, Victorian British accent. At this point, I wasn't sure which person was Richard's uncle.

The gentleman with Swahili accent introduced himself as Oscar, the uncle of my friend Richard. As previously stated, he didn't look anything like I'd imagined. He was very pale skinned with heavy, fine grayish-white hair that gave him a very distinct almost southern European look.

We then entered an older model red Peugeot. The second gentleman turned around and introduced himself as Mr. Lance de Silva. He was a slight, balding man with dreamy kind eyes. His attire looked like something out of the British Victorian age and seemed somewhat out of place in the Kenyan weather, nevertheless, it gave him a unique individual style and look.

We drove the crowded streets of Nairobi. I was almost taken aback by the number of street children who approached the cars, oblivious to any rules of traffic or consideration. As with my first trip to Kenya, I immediately sensed the underlying current of anger and dissatisfaction on the faces of the people in the streets of Nairobi.

As we passed the crowded angry streets of inner city Nairobi, we slowly progressed into the narrow, hilly roadside of the suburbs lined with kiosks, small wooden shops, selling everything from calling cards to flashlights. Moving into the plush area of Kilaleshwa, I sensed the wide social disparity between the upper and lower classes. I could immediately feel the aloof sense of privilege coming from the people who I observed in this upper-class suburb. Surely, in the United States and other countries that I have visited, there was a dividing line between social classes. However, this was my first experience of observing it so openly and tangible.

Living in Kenya was stepping back into time, at least on the social and political landscapes. Although Kenya is much more developed than many other Sub-Saharan African nations, its social structure was archaic in my eyes. It was lost in the years of British colonialism, of an all-powerful Indian merchant class, and a despotic and inefficiently run black government.

The year that I relocated to Nairobi, Kenya, was also the year that the winds of change were beginning to blow the decrepit and decadent halls of corruption beneath Kenya's weak foundation of stability and mask of democracy. It was truly an exciting time to come to Kenya, as the old guardsmen and dictator president was on the way out. As I arrived in Mr. Oscar's home, I was overwhelmed at how large the yard was. It truly looked like a scene out of an old movie such as *Out of Africa*. It was breathtakingly beautiful; almost surreal. There were orange trees everywhere. I could actually hear myself think, which ironically is a luxury in many parts of Africa. In that space, I almost began to lose myself and travel back in time to a place where adventurers such as Ernest Hemingway would find the essence of their being in the wild breezes of remote Africa.

Two seconds later, a small boy of mixed African/Arab ancestry approached me. He greeted me in Swahili saying *habari*. I smiled and answered *habari*. I then asked him what his name was, he replied very enthusiastically, Adam! We instantly bonded. He said, "I want to show you where the new clubhouse is located." Just as we were walking down a narrow pathway right inside the yard, a youngish looking Somali woman came out of the door and called his name.

"Adam, Adam!" He ran in her direction with total abandonment, and I assumed that this must be the nanny of the house with whom he had a very close relationship. I then introduced myself, and she responded very reticently, "Habari." And she stated, "my name is Raga." To my utter shock, I then heard Adam call her mommy! I couldn't believe my ears. Oscar who was every bit of seventy-five or older, had a young six-year-old son by a woman who was no more that twenty-five? Again in Africa, the profane and the sacred often merge on every level.

After finally settling in my room, I realized that I had left one of my luggage bags back in the hotel. I spoke with Oscar, and he suggested that we go first thing in the morning to retrieve it. I can remember this sleepless night, the uneasiness that I had in the pit of my stomach. It wasn't simply the baggage that was left at the hotel, but the overall feeling of discontentment with Kenya. I rationalized in my head that it was far too early to make any judgment on an entire country based on a few early experiences. If there is anything that I learned living in Africa, I knew I had to trust the little voice inside. Here intuition reigns supreme; logic isn't king here. As previously stated, this is often the greatest obstacle to Westerners trying to make sense of Sub-Saharan Africa. It can be really frustrating for foreign businesspeople who come here and try to be movers and shakers.

The next morning we climbed into an old beat red Peugeot and set off to the 369 Hotel in downtown Nairobi. As we entered the hotel, I went directly towards the front desk, which was amazingly empty this day. I spoke to a young Kikuyu lady, thin with neat braids and frigid, calculating eyes. I explained to her that I had just checked out of room 507 yesterday and that I forgot a black carry-on bag. She seemed to know what I was speaking of, yet still, she refused to give me any eye contact and also seemed visibly irritated at my presence. She told us to wait for the manager who would be back in about ten minutes. We sat there, and my mind slightly wondered off. The dilapidated upholstery used to decorate the hotel was really hard to the eyes. I thought about how inefficient the management was here and how would this staff fare if it were in the United States. I silently smiled to myself and began to catch on to my own imperialistic biases buried deep in my own unconscious thoughts.

Twenty minutes later, I was approached by two Kenyan detectives who showed me their badges and then asked me to accompany them to the police station. In utter shock, I asked them to explain why. Oscar must have detected the growing hostility in my voice as he intervened and told both officers that he was coming with us.

We arrived at what looked like a rundown Boy Scout Clubhouse. The outside of the building was constructed of a hideous mixture of dilapidated wood and cement, and was in need of a serious paint job. The lighting inside the building was dim. As we entered the main room where the bookings took place, a very large and imposing dark man wearing a semi-paramilitary uniform greeted us. He sat back as if he was enjoying our sense of fear and uncertainty. This seemed to be a common attribute within some divisions of the Kenyan police, to display a false sense of power in order to extort bribes. As we sat there, the officer asked me what I was doing in Kenya in a very condescending, self-satisfied way. This process of intimidation was very pervasive throughout Kenya, particularly during the Moi administration.

We sat there in this petty chief's office for over an hour as my friend Oscar discussed many of his old acquaintances within the Kenyan police department. I assumed at this point that he was used to harassment by the Kenyan police, and this was one of the coping mechanisms. I, on the other hand, was totally inexperienced and was actually very annoyed that this was taking place, especially under such false pretenses.

After an hour, we were finally released to go our way. I must admit that I was not only livid, but I was somehow deeply disturbed by this lack of honor and concept of corruption within the authority. These are things that the average Westerner only reads about in the newspaper or watches on his or her television set during the six o'clock news. The actual reality is a much rawer, disempowering, and scary situation. I can only imagine the sense of isolation and impotence that a person feels when they grow up in a society like this. For all of my disenchantment with the United States, I have always felt that there was a way of rectifying wrongs there both legally and politically. However, Kenya was another world. It was a place that was steeped in a dark veil of corruption and immorality. It was a system that seemed engrossed in deep nepotism, ethnic and tribal loyalties, and very localized and parochial worldviews. My bag was finally returned to me.

That evening, I was unable to sleep, still perplexed by the accusations and wondering what the meaning of the entire ordeal was. There I was half awake, half asleep, wondering and worrying about my first day at work with the Refugee Resettlement Organization. In my mind, I wondered if this lack of honor was a cultural reflection that would also permeate this organization.

The morning brought with it the rising sun, the chirping of birds, and a deep knot in the pit of my stomach. It was like the feeling that I would get as a young child afraid to go to school because I had not done my homework, or like the sense of guilt that engulfed me when I was forced to go to church on Sunday mornings by my mother after having a particularly sinful Saturday!

I left with Oscar, accompanied by Lance De Silva. We dropped Oscar's son off first at a local primary school. Lance began to tell the story of the old British school where he was a head instructor for some years. His sense of nostalgia for the old days made him sound like an old British colonial master looking for the time when the sun never set on the British Empire. Surprisingly I actually found him quite entertaining. He was so influenced and engrossed with everything British that I truly believed that he forgot that he was of Indian ancestry. Even with his strong cultural disconnect, there was something engaging, charming, and innocent in his countenance. I was really curious to know why he felt such a joy identifying with Western imperialism. What was it that gave him a sense of security and well-being in their colonial social stratification? Maybe it was the sweet feeling of childhood innocence that engulfed him during the days of his youth? Maybe it was the fond memories of childhood that prodded him in this direction, a selfish sentimentalism which held supreme realms upon his unconsciousness?

Driving down dirt roads that seemed lined for miles with small kiosks, small local shops that catered to the local populace, we approached the compound. It looked ominous and cold, almost similar to some of the maximum-security prisons in the US. Kenyan guards were all over the place carrying AK-47s along with a faraway deadened look in their eyes.

As I entered the gate, I was overcome with the worst feeling in my stomach. It seemed like I was walking into a realm of unhappiness, betrayal, and entrapment. I caught myself and said that this had to be a figment of my imagination, a warped fear that was resurfacing in this moment of truth. I greeted the lady at the front desk. She was a small Kenyan, short, slender, with very prominent eyes and a high forehead. She smiled and spoke English in a very thick Kenyan accent. However, behind her engaging smile were cold eyes which certainly weren't smiling. It was as if her smile was masking more sinister intentions.

A Kenyan named Paul gave me a mini-tour. He was a slight man around twenty-five years old, with keen aquiline features. He could have easily passed for an Ethiopian or Somali. He was very soft-spoken and had an easy demeanor that conveyed that he was used to socializing with foreigners. I was taken to a small office upstairs and then introduced to two ladies who would be my trainers. Amisha was a rather nerdy-looking Somali girl with thick glasses and a typically prominent forehead. Her demeanor was very harsh and standoffish. The other woman was a thickset, dark-skinned Kenyan named Masani. She was much more engaging than Amisha. She had an easy smile and very kind, sensitive eyes. She asked me where I was from in the States, and I told her Philadelphia. She gave me a somewhat pensive look and then asked me if that was near California. I started laughing and said that it was actually on the opposite end of the country. She apologized and mentioned that the communications director of the organization used to live in California. It seemed that over half of the caseworkers here from the US were from California.

I was given a study package and told that I should take it in the back room just to review and get more detailed insight into the type of work that we would be doing in the field. As I sat in the back room for over twenty minutes, a very large, heavyset white American woman who seemed to be having a tough time both walking and breathing approached me. Our eyes met, and we both said hello, and she then extended her hand out and introduced herself as Maggie. She stepped back and looked at me really hard and said, "please be careful in this organization, this place doesn't like African American males!" I was totally taken back! Here I was in the middle of Africa listening to a white American woman warn me about racism. It all seemed almost surreal; I can distinctly remember simply sitting there and almost laughing to myself at the irony of the whole situation.

As I looked into Maggie's eyes, I could see the sincerity in her need to share the injustices that she had witnessed within this organization. And yet there was something in me that hoped that she was greatly exaggerating. As I sat there looking into her eyes, I could see the sincerity and genuine concern. This scared me more than anything else. For the rest of the day, I wandered around the grounds trying to get a feel, to get an intuitive picture of what life is going to be like working here.

That entire evening, I was again unable to sleep after Maggie's comments. I just kept trying to analyze in my head how and why there would be a proliferation of hostile feelings against black American men here. Maggie's words kept playing in my mind like a ferris wheel, reaching its paramount and then just freezing there in my mind, tormenting and intimidating in height and then descending once again into the realms of logical skepticism.

The next day, I reported to the junior manager Mary Green. She was a heavyset woman with fair skin, dark curly hair, and she spoke with a laid-back Midwestern accent. She could have easily passed for an Arab or Hispanic. She had a coarse, harsh, and almost rude demeanor. As I walked in, she refused to give me any eye contact. She then decided to have a conversation on the phone while I sat and listened. I guess this was her way of humiliating me and showing her dominance and control from the beginning.

She hung up the phone, and I then introduced myself. She still refused to look up, but proceeded to go directly into the details of the job. Towards the end of her information, she then stated that they check everyone's background for criminal activity.

I gave her a condescending smirk and simply nodded my head in confidence. This was certainly a strong foreshadowing of challenging situations to come.

Later that afternoon, I had an appointment to get my utilities turned on in my new apartment. There was a tall white gentleman named Troy who was also a caseworker within the organization. He was a tall man with long hair and a seemingly bad attitude. He reminded me of someone who was stuck in the late sixties or early seventies, a rebel without a cause so to speak. As I would later find out, although Troy was somewhat rude and rough around the edges, he also had a very generous heart and always seemed to keep his word, the latter being a rarity in Kenya.

As I went to the utility department, a ten-minute wait turned into almost an hour. This caused me to arrive back to work about twenty minutes late. I immediately went into the office and talked to my supervisor to let her know why I was running late. She seemed really okay with it and explained that this type of slow inconsiderate service was the staple of Kenyan culture.

I was then introduced to my trainer, an austere-looking Somali/Kenyan lady named Ameena. She was aloof, self-absorbed, and had an elderly aura that made her look twice her age. I shook her hand and introduced myself. She then asked if I was Muslim. I gave my usual smile and ambiguous answer. She was a little confused by my response. She inquired more, "what do you mean sort of? Either you are, or you're not." I sat back and contemplated why religion was so important in Kenya's culture. It seemed just as important as the concept of race in the US.

I honestly believe that it goes back to this communal mindset, which helps the individual survive the tough and harsh realities that have now so afflicted many parts of Africa. However, what Kenya needs more than ever is a sense of its own being, a feeling of perspective of its own cultural and historical significance.

From my experiences, there seems to be a great emphasis placed on doctrine and the literal interpretation of the law as opposed to the spirit of religions. Areas that are primarily Muslim appear to foster a unified consciousness that identifies with Arabism and gain a sense of importance by believing themselves to be blessed by the grace of Allah and the identification with a Middle Eastern worldview and culture—which, according to them, is more civilized and advanced than anything traditionally African. Many African Christians, on the other hand, believe that they have the Western cultural privilege into modernity, and create a sense of alienation by defining both Islamic and Indigenous traditions as being backward and barbaric. There was a sense of exclusivity that comes from their identification with the European culture ethos, and all of the perceived historical advancement that belonged to it.

Many Kenyans would be in complete denial that their religion was anything other than a direct link to the Almighty, a connection into the truth of the universal matters; not that their beliefs are basically the residue of colonial Arab and European domination.

After work, I decided to explore the Nairobi nightlife with my fellow co-worker Troy, who was also known as the Jesus of Nairobi because of his long hair, tall height, and white skin. We met up around 8 p.m. and headed straight to a Club Florida in a small suburb of the city. The club was full of Indian Kenyans all gathered together, too self-conscious and inept to try dancing. They desperately tried to avoid mixing with other groups, especially the black Africans. This was my first encounter with the level of insularity of the Indian community in Kenya. It would certainly not be my last. There was a great divide between the Kenyan African and Indian communities on a myriad of different levels; socially, politically, economically, and almost every other level of human dynamic imaginable. It was almost as if the Indians in Kenya were living in a separate reality, completely removed from any genuine human interactions with their black African counterparts. However, this divide wasn't just limited to the division between Indians and Africans, but there was also a profound disconnect found between black Africans themselves. As previously mentioned, the largest tribe in Kenya, the Kikuyu, dominated every aspect of the economic and political life. The Luo, the tribe which President Obama's father comes from, is regionally known as the intellectuals, lawyers, and scholars of Kenya.

We sat there until the wee hours of the night listening to old American eighties music and laughing as I observed a group of Asian Kenyans attempting to dance to the lethargic tunes. As the night passed away, I began to hear a deep melancholy in Troy's voice. He was very bitter at life and seemed to be hiding in this country and behind this line of work as a way to forget his past or to recreate himself. Maybe like many of us, he was seeking to heal or reinvent who he was. In the short period, it became clear to me that the majority of the expats working here all seemed to have a rather tragic reason for coming to Kenya. Each of us had stories to tell, some sordid, others much less intense.

The next day was anti-climatic in comparison. I went out of my small apartment to go food shopping. I walked through what seemed to be a pool of spilled over sewage. The smell mixed with sweet jacaranda flowers would forever taint my senses regarding Nairobi. The aroma indelibly colored my memories of here, memories wrapped in both beautiful and ugly experiences, whispers that will forever remain in my consciousness, like vague shadows seen but never truly understood.

On Monday morning, I was summoned to the supervisor's office around 9 a.m. I was a little shocked, but I just figured that it was an informational meeting. As I would soon find out, it was more of a reprimand. The supervisor, a Mrs. Tisha Moshena, was rarely seen by us case workers, and when she was, she seemed to be operating on a level of tension and uneasiness. She started off asking, "is everything going well with your apartment and moving process?" For a split second, I thought she was showing genuine concern and interest. However, after about a minute, I could see the resentment in her eyes, the insincerity of her smile, and the condescension in her tone. I was totally at a loss for words. I was in disbelief that she was actually trying to chastise me for coming back to work twenty minutes late after knowing full well what my dilemma was. I just thought to myself that this was the height of unprofessionalism and seemed to reek of a personal affront. My mind wandered back thinking of what Maggie warned me about on my first day on the job. Was there really an anti-black American conspiracy working throughout the organization?

I clearly articulated that I had notified Marsha of what was transpiring before I went and she had given me the okay. Trisha said, "well, that's not what I was apprised of."

At this point, I was becoming a little agitated. I simply stated my case again and said it was a mistake. I think my tone let her know in so many words that I was ready to move on and didn't feel any guilt as to what had transpired. Although it was a fairly small conflict, it just revealed that there were personal feelings involved and fairness wasn't going to be the menu of the day.

As I went to the mall that day, I listened to the voice of a tall brown-skinned, lost-looking man who seemed to be whispering on the Internet café phone. "What am I supposed to do now?" He asked. I briefly thought that he was Kenyan, being that he was speaking a mixture of broken Kiswahili and English. We briefly made eye contact and he asked, "are you American?" I smiled slightly and asked how he knew. He stated in a heavy Southern drawl, "I could tell by your independent demeanor." I laughed and asked him to elaborate."

"Well, most Kenyans seem to have to be around someone always. It's almost taboo to be alone or by oneself in Africa. You're also quite hairy for an African!" I was shocked at this statement. I was never really that conscious of my hairiness until coming to Africa. I then looked around and noticed that the majority of black Kenyans hardly had any body hair. I was acutely aware of this physical attribute. This physical feature comes from my father's side of the family. They are somewhat mixed, with claims of being Native American. In reality, I believe that the ancestry is most likely European/Jewish.

I began to feel consciously more American, more isolated, and more removed from the continental indigenous culture in which I wanted to immerse myself. Not only because of the physical attributes but also the psychological and mental ones as well. One of the issues was that I felt just as far removed from my countrymen, particularly my white American co-workers. Ironically, I connected mostly to the refugees that I was here to help process. I completely empathize with their plight. For I too also felt like someone without a home, of course not to the same degree or conditions as those they were forced to leave. The emotional and mental resentment that comes with knowing that one can never be fully accepted and embraced in the land of one's birth simply because of color or race sets up a wall of separation and an inner disconnect that can never truly be reconciled.

I finally had the chance to meet with one of the male Afro-American case workers named Regi. At this time, I had a million and one questions to ask him. After our eyes had met, I asked him, "what brings you to Nairobi?"

"Travel and self-discovery."

I laughed and told him that I was on the same journey. All of a sudden I had a mini-memory recall. This guy's name was fairly infamous within the organization. His cases were sarcastically called Regi cases, and each one had to be reevaluated because of his perceived incompetence.

"I've been here a year too long and will be going back to Alabama with my wife."

I told him that I was looking to rent an apartment as soon as possible.

"Our apartment is up for rent. Come and have a look."

After work, we took the minibus to Regi's apartment which was relatively close to the large mall popular with many expats. We went down a hill into the gated apartment complex. The door opened, and his wife Jane came out and greeted us in broken English.

"Hello, how are you. I am Jane." She was statuesque, tall, muscular, with smooth dark brown skin and almond-shaped jumping jet black eyes.

"Hello, my name is Hassan," I answered.

"Where are you from?"

"The States, New Jersey to be exact."

"Oh really? It's funny. There aren't that many Afro-Americans here in Kenya. It seems that most of them are more interested in going to West and South Africa. What brought you specifically to Kenya?"

I smiled at her and told her work-related circumstances. I mentioned that I previously lived in Tanzania and actually preferred to work there.

I then asked Jane if she was from Kenya. With a very strong no, and a knowing pride, she let me know that she was from Uganda. I told her that I was in Uganda once, when I first arrived in Kenya. It was a very enlightening experience. We visited a city called Jinja, considered by many to be the very source of the Nile. It had a semi-surreal feeling to it. A very strong spiritual energy surrounded the place.

I asked Jane if she preferred Uganda to Kenya, and she simply looked at me as if I had lost my mind. "Kenyans are not good people," she said. "There are exceptions to the rule, but in general, Ugandans are very honest people."

I laughed slightly. "Well, Jane you can't generalize an entire nation. However, I must say that with some of my recent experiences, I would have to concur with your opinion."

We all burst out laughing.

After being shown a mini tour of the apartment, I decided that this possibly could be a good place to settle. One drawback was that there weren't many other foreigners living there. This would be an advantage in the long run. In this field, one really has to get away from the constant pressures of work and all its related politics. Within the humanitarian/ journalist field, it's vital to be able to have your own personal space, an escape route so to speak.

There was one small problem, however. The window in the back room was busted. It seemed strange for Jane and Regi to allow something like this to remain unfixed for so long. After I had questioned them about the window, Jane replied, "one of the neighbor's children kicked a ball and broke it, and now we are in the process of getting it resolved."

I said that I would be interested in taking the apartment under on condition; the window had to be fixed by the perpetrators.

The next day I went to work with the feeling that I held a little secret, a sense that I was able to function in Nairobi without being completely connected or involved with work.

I then decided to snoop around a bit after listening to what I'd heard about many of the people in the organization. My perception had begun to change. My demeanor became much more reserved. I observed the subtle hypocrisy that is often so measurably tangible in the world of development workers. Many people are very unaware of this attitude. There is very often the false sense of liberalism that permeates the cultural undercurrent. There were actual cases marked Regi cases! I couldn't for the life of me understand how this could be. The irony was that this somewhat experienced case worker was so incompetent that his cases had to be reviewed by other less experienced caseworkers to ensure that they were up to par before being processed. It bewildered me how an agency could hire someone if he or she had a severe learning disability.

I left work early that day to prepare for my move to Regi's place. My mind was hardly at peace. I kept thinking about the negative condemnations that the organization had towards him. I traveled thousands of miles away from my homeland only to find the same breed of not so subtle racism veering its ugly head. That afternoon, I went to the nearest mall to check my email. I was going to meet Regi here in an hour and figured that this would be a good way to burn time. What seemed like a harmless excursion, turned out to be a real disaster.

We met at the mall and discussed the details of getting the window fixed. As we walked back to his place, he pointed to a man wearing an all-white *galibaya* and an Islamic cap as the father of the culprit. "This was the father of the boy who broke the window some months ago. He refuses to have it fixed." At this point, I thought that I should try to intercede. I approached the gentleman and attempted to tell him that I was going to be the new tenant in the apartment and was curious to know how and why the window was broken. Before I could get another word out of my mouth, he charged after me with a bat. Well, all hell broke loose. I then proceeded to pick up a large stick to defend myself. We literally circled and yelled at one another in the middle of the apartment complex. During the entire fiasco, I felt how silly this must have looked to all of the neighbors who came out to witness where all of the chaos and noise was coming from. Eventually, several neighbors came to investigate and break up the fight. Slightly embarrassed, I felt justified in my actions. After all, I was only defending myself and possibly my life. Regi looked more upset and shaken than I did.

"Hassan, maybe you should go lay low for the day until things calm down."

I then left and went over to the local mall to check my email. I ordered a cup of tea hoping that it would help me to lower my adrenaline and calm my temper. After about twenty minutes, I received a message on my cell phone marked urgent. As I looked closer, I saw that it was from Regi. I was a little provoked as I knew that the message was about the recent altercation. My first instinct was to simply go home and wait out this issue until the next day. Well, my ego and sense of justice made me go back to confront whoever wanted to know about the situation. As I approached the apartment complex, I saw a group of people surrounding Regi's apartment. I was approached by two Kenyan police officers in plain clothes who asked me to come with them to the police station. I was irate. First of all, I yelled out you didn't even ask me for my version of the story! They took me in the police car to a dilapidated station which seemed like it was a million miles away. During this voyage, the officer kept asking me to apologize! By this time, I was in full rebellion mode. I absolutely refused to apologize for something that was not my fault. In the back of my mind, I knew that this was some sort of set up. I had it in my mind that I would refuse to apologize since I knew that I did nothing wrong. I was taken to a cold, unfurnished office with a rather young-looking police officer with frigid, dead eyes. He seemed to be enjoying his power, his authority, and his sense of getting even with the West. I was just as determined not to give an inch, not to give him the satisfaction of an apology, not to allow him to feel the power which he was so desperately seeking.

As I sat there in the cold, sterile, small room looking in the eyes of this petty dictator who despite me being black, still felt as if he was getting even with his imperial masters. Of course, it was much easier for him to take this out on someone who looked more like himself, as opposed to the many European and white American NGO workers in the country. After I was detained in this small dust-filled room for over an hour, suddenly there was a loud knock at the door. I could hear a group of people assembling outside, which seemed to make the officer somewhat uncomfortable. Ten minutes later, a tall, dark, very distinguished gentleman from the housing complex arrived. He identified himself as a policeman and as a primary witness stated that I was innocent in this entire incident. I was both relieved and shocked at the same time. My optimism would be short lived. The police officer was still showing unreasonable intransigence and blatant disregard for the law and the truth. He even refused to accommodate what a fellow officer was saying. He didn't want to hear an objective view from a fellow law officer. It was at this moment that I recognized the severity and depth of Kenyan corruption.

I sat in that uncomfortable chair until the wee hours of the morning. I had my supervisor call the police station at which time I was immediately released.

The next day, I was the laughing stock at work. My colleagues jokingly called me convict! I had a meeting with Elizabeth, who was the blonde-haired director of the US resettlement organization here in Kenya. She sat me down and stated, "well, I need to be honest with you. For some reason, these incidents seem to happen to a lot of Afro-Americans within our program. Unfortunately, as a white woman, I am treated like royalty in Kenya."

I calmly smiled, but inside I seethed with resentment. The reality, although exasperating, was hard to deny. There was certainly a double standard in Kenya when it came to race, and the blacks were on the short end of the stick. It was amazing that I traveled this far to escape racism only to find its rear at me with vengeance. Like some twisted long lost friend, she offered not only a sense of frustration, but also a sick sense of familiarity.

Our first assignment was a two-week excursion in Ethiopia to process Eritrean refugees. Ethiopia was stunningly beautiful, a land of ancient contrasts; both old and modern, compassionate yet harsh, materialistic yet deeply spiritual, and rigidly traditional yet profoundly progressive!

We arrived on time at the massive Hilton Hotel that was located in the heart of its capital, Addis Ababa. Driving from the airport, I was overtaken by the sheer natural beauty of Ethiopia; its rolling green hills, beautifully dressed exotic women, along with its austere and disciplined police officers. As we drove through the hilly city, somewhat reminiscent of California's Bay area, I was amazed at how organized and clean the streets were in comparison to Nairobi. There was a dignity, pride, and sense of self-respect that seemed to be lacking in Nairobi. As an Afro-American, it was enriching and empowering to experience such a feast of cultural dignity and historical pride.

As we pulled into the Hilton Hotel, the other members of the team greeted us. The first person who got my attention was a young lady named Fania. She was a wealthy Cuban American with a brash in-your-face type of personality that, according to office gossip, was not in good favor with the majority of our coworkers. First impressions can be lasting if one isn't interested in exploring the deeper essential motives behind a behavior. I often live by the credo that the entire world is a giant stage, and everyone is wearing his or her personal mask.

As we pulled into the hotel, I was amazed at the number of foreigners occupying it. As with most countries in Sub-Saharan Africa, the massive financial investments always seemed to come from outside of the boundaries of the continent. Some may look at this as tangible evidence of a global neo-colonial economic system. Others simply blame the ineptitude of the African leaders themselves. I am under the impression that it's a mixture of both. Western countries support many of these corrupt and so-called inept leaders, as long as they, in turn, support Western interests.

In the hotel, a beautiful Ethiopian hostess took us to our rooms. She was tall, thin, with very thick hair, and she spoke with a rich, deep, accent. She was shy, yet did not seem innocent. After taking me to my room, she lingered and gave me prolonged eye contact. This often translates into an aggressive posture in these parts. It reminds me of the same mysterious attraction that one would experience in Zanzibar with the Arab women who were covered with a full galabaya, but whose eyes could speak volumes.

There is often a very subtle way of starting relationships in Ethiopia and Kenya. Here the eyes are not only the mirror of the soul but also the power of the mouth. In this culture, there were many different forms of communication besides the spoken word. Dance and rhythm take on the highest form of expression. Here rhythm seems to be the code of communication in the development between the persons. In the West, we often overlook or rather undervalue the concept of non-verbal communication. Our primary mode of communication is often superficial and often linear. Within the Swahili and Amharic languages, there are definite emphases on bonding with people on a myriad of levels. As mentioned earlier, the entire linguistic dynamic functions with the goal of connecting with the other person. This deeply contrasts with the detached objectivity of European languages such as English.

The next morning, I again bumped into Fania at breakfast. She was exuberant to have someone that knew a little about her culture. We sat down and started to recap about Cuban culture in particular Santeria. She was deeply anti-Castro, like most white privileged Cubans. The more I spoke with her, the more I realized how conservative and impressed with the western status quo she was. I was perplexed as to why someone with her mindset and political leanings would choose to work and live in Kenya. There's an old saying in Latin America: the culture loves and nourishes its mother (Africa), but admires and aspires to be like its father (Europe). Nevertheless, I found her to be refreshingly frank and sincere. Fania had a passion and naïveté that was lacking in many of the other more nuanced and cunning coworkers. She had a wonderful lack of pretension, which was so prevalent within the NGO culture. Her brutal honesty was refreshing.

This was the first day that I finally started working with the refugees. We began by processing Eritrean refugees who claimed to have been abused and discriminated against in Ethiopia. Physically we couldn't distinguish between the two groups. Even linguistically they sounded very similar. As an Afro-American, and maybe more importantly as a human being, to see so much inter-tribal friction and polarization was disturbing. Ironically with all of the poverty, political, social, as well as economic divisions that can be found here, this was one of the noblest and hospitable societies that I have ever visited. Ethiopia's generosity was sincere and transparent. The air here was clean and crisp, a mountain drop background that encapsulates the mind.

The ancient monuments here are astoundingly underrated and truly enriching to anyone of African descent or simply anyone with a penchant for history. I visited some of the ancient Coptic churches as well as the burial tomb of Haile Selassie, considered one of the modern founders of the nation. Unfortunately, our time in Ethiopia was going to be short lived and very limited. Between working eight hours and six days in the limited amount of time of seven days, there wasn't a lot of time to explore all that Ethiopia had to offer.

Our first day at work in Addis Ababa was very challenging. I was assigned to Amina the Kenyan Somali trainer. We had a trying synergy right from the start. I found her to be impersonal and abrupt. In the beginning, I thought that maybe she was simply somewhat reticent because she didn't know me. I would later find out that she was an intolerant and outright mean person. As we talked to the refugees, I noticed her condescending and almost hostile attitude toward them. She would also make very negative comments about the majority of the people being processed.

Unfortunately, this attitude was pervasive among many of the black African relief workers. So deeply embedded was the uneven social dynamic that it penetrated the very depths of the non-profit world in which upper-class, educated Africans worked. This was a tremendous insight, as well as a great disappointment to the world in which I had thrown myself in with idealistic eyes.

That evening I was quietly contemplating the day and trying to understand the unequal relationships that existed within this society. As I lay in my bed that evening, I was awakened by a knock at the door. To my surprise, it was Fania, the Cuban girl who I had just met a couple of days ago. She was upset and frazzled. I was actually afraid for her. She slowly opened the door, and I let her in the room. Her eyes were bloodshot from crying so much. She told me that she was having an affair with one of the United Nations workers who she later found out was married.

Promiscuity was rampant throughout the development industry. This would be one of many forms of outright hypocrisy and double standards in the expression of moral behavior that I found to be pervasive in the world of NGOs.

I had to remain focused on my goals and not become discouraged by the intrinsic duplicity of my work. In my heart, I was still working as a journalist, and I realized that this was simply a step in getting the most objective experiential story possible.

That was actually my first real encounter with refugees that were being resettled. It was my first real involvement with the world of international migration. It put an actual face and made theory tangible to the human experience and expression. In the beginning, the stories were most painful. The sheer shock of hearing the profoundly inhuman behavior that people are capable of inflicting on each other is overwhelming during the first stages of the work. I went off to work with more vigor and a deep sense of mission that I could somehow make a profound impact on the lives of these individuals.

That evening I thought about the situation of many of the refugees with whom I worked. It really made me reflect on my own life, struggles, and time, and gave me a deep appreciation of the blessings into which I was born. I have often complained about being born black in the United States, but I have never experienced anything as traumatizing at this. It's amazing how many perspectives life can show you, how many levels of reality that can engulf your senses. One really can begin to wonder what it would be like not to be able to travel home, to ever see family again. Being an exiled gypsy can be liberating, but at the same time destabilizing and disorienting. One refugee I know described it much like being a ghost; invisible, insignificant, unworthy, lost, and belonging nowhere. I was temporary exiled based on my own choice, which is so different from being legally forced to leave one's home and being unable to return.

The day ended with all of us going hiking in the nearby mountains and eating traditional Ethiopian food. For a country that has seen so much suffering and war, Ethiopia was truly a warm and welcoming country.

The following week we headed back to Nairobi. It was a huge let down in comparison to the civility of Ethiopia. Working within the home office was completely different from working out in the field. The level of racism that existed here was appalling. I was warned on my first day, and I did get to experience its ugly but familiar face up close and personal. The majority of the local Africans who worked with us didn't earn nearly as much as their Western counterparts, nor did they have the same influence that we had within the organization.

Our first week back was fairly mundane. We were all working together, pulling files for refugees' cases. It was truly drugging work. Ironically, a tangible hierarchy was also very much a part of this organization and deeply reflected the great disparity between the local workers and the foreign staff. The American staff often worked within the comfortable confines of the air-conditioned office. Our hours were shorter, our work less strenuous, and our salaries much higher. I found this extremely disturbing and disheartening. The longer that I worked within the NGO world, the more disillusioned I became. The very same racism and oppression that some NGO's set out to combat seemed to permeate the very core of their organizations. This core racism also seemed to drive the fabric in which they operated. I was still trying to find my original idealism, to be centered on the higher notion of humanitarian vision, and to recapture the passion that allowed me to travel a thousand miles to unknown territory in order to find myself. However, the reality began to shatter my perspective. I felt as if I was drowning in a dream world of neo-colonialism.

At the end of the work week, I went to eat at a local Somali restaurant in my neighborhood. After a month of eating the local Kenyan staple of *ugali* and *yama*, African meat and potatoes, I was in search for something more exotic and tasty. I entered a small hall in the wall building and was led to the upstairs by a very elegant and attractive Somali lady. She was tall, bronze skinned, with long, silky flowing black hair. A few long curls were escaping from her thick hair loosely gathered at the back of her head and held by a sizable red-colored braid that gently fell over her shoulders. As she moved closer, I was slightly surprised at how muscular and slender she was. As she reached over to set the table, I immediately saw her gold bracelets with an ivory inlay that she wore on her graceful wrist and smoothed brown arms and also the large, impressive, and unusual rings on two fingers of her right hand. All these contrasted with the simple elegance of her outfit which consisted of cream colored trousers and a loose, white combed-cotton blouse. They were like natural extensions of her body, the parts that she could never hide. I had not yet been able to look into her eyes. I would see them when she brought the food out from the kitchen and placed it on the table.

Her eyes were a deep brown, enveloped by long black lashes, large in relation to her face. They were more than just mere eyes. In her eyes, I saw a distant land. Her eyes were a mirror of her spirit, so sad, yet composed, mysterious, and rebellious. I asked myself if I thought she was beautiful—yes, but there was something more than just her beauty. She left me with an altogether different feeling, a sense that to even ask the question is ridiculous and should not be asked. I even began to question myself, maybe my impression of her extraordinary beauty was just a delusion. The suspense was killing me. She came back bringing a plate of goat meat and rice, cooked with a special Somali sauce. There was a low melodic Arabic sounding music playing in the background. I sat outside on this unusually warm evening, being engulfed by the alluring, vibrant, and erotic smells of musk and sandalwood incense. Upon finishing the meal and receiving the bill, I wanted to stall time in order to have a deeper conversation with her. Finally, towards the end of the evening, I mustered up enough courage to speak more casually with her.

"I'm sorry but what is your name?"

"My name is Fazia. Why are you sorry?" She asked smiling again. She spoke elegantly and had an easy sensuous demeanor. "And what is your name?"

"Hassan," I answered.

"Hassan, are you Muslim?"

"Well not really, I sort of embrace all religions."

She looked utterly perplexed at this point. She just stood there staring at me but smiling the entire time. Suddenly, everything seemed unreal and baffling. I fell silent, not knowing how to continue the conversation, unsure whether I should continue or not. Fazia gently touched my hand and said, "It's as though I know your face from somewhere. Where are you from?"

"The US."

"And why in the world are you in Nairobi?"

To tell the truth, at that moment my being there amazed me just as much as it did her. "I'm a journalist and aid worker."

"Maybe that's why you look familiar to me; I've seen you on TV."

And we both burst out into laughter.

The more she spoke, the more comfortable I became in getting to know her. I then asked where she was from.

"Obviously Somalia, but I grew up in Uganda and Kenya."

Uganda? I was a little taken aback by this answer. "May I ask how you ended up in Uganda from Somalia?"

"My family has its origins in Hargeisa, Somalia. This used to be British Somalia. I come from a family of medical doctors and professors. My father was killed during our country's civil war, and my family had to flee. First through Kenya and then into Uganda."

"Why didn't your family just stay in Nairobi like so many Somali refugees?" I asked.

"That is exactly the point, Hassan, there were already so many Somalis here that my mother refused to simply have her family disappear into a sea of despair and begging. My mother is a trained nurse and has a lot of experience working with the sick. At the time, Uganda seemed to be much more open to giving opportunities to educated Somalis than Kenya. She found work in an AIDS orphanage outside of Kampala."

"Is she still working there?"

"Yes, but only part time. I have five little siblings at home, and our status as refugees forbids us from working full time either in Uganda or Kenya. Nevertheless, mom is very dedicated to the orphanage."

"That is really amazing that your mom has such deep-seated compassion and dedication to serving others."

"Yes, it is, and if there were more like her many parts of Africa wouldn't be like they are today."

"I am still confused why you're in Nairobi and not back home in Uganda?"

"Simple. I can make more money in Kenya doing odd jobs than working full time in Uganda! I live with relatives, so I don't have to pay for rent, and I spent very little for food."

Fazia looked pensive and then became silent. I figured that maybe I asked too many penetrating questions and needed to back off a bit. She asked me if I would like another cup of tea to break the tension and then disappeared into the back kitchen for what seemed like an eternity. As she came out with the tea, I saw that she was smiling again and had the same warm inviting look which initially drew me to want to know her better. This time she actually sat down beside me and looked intently into my eyes. "If you could cover any story in Kenya right now, what would it be?"

I said that I was very interested in knowing more about the elections coming up soon. She laughed and said, "yes, you've come during a critical time in Kenya's history."

I asked her what she meant by that. There have always been elections in Kenya, yet the current president, Moi, stayed in power for almost a decade.

"Yes, silly, this is exactly the point. For the first time, there is a real chance of change here."

I asked, "what makes you so sure this time around?"

"Oh, there is real change and discontent in the air. I also have some journalist friends who have some insights into the inner workings of how things work here. I am surprised that you're still so skeptical. Being a journalist with the United Nations, you should know these things."

I looked at her back just as intently and stated, "I've been here only over two months and have been seemingly betrayed at every level."

"I wouldn't exactly call it a betrayal. It's simply that you don't actually understand how the Kenyan system works. You have to know someone in every aspect of life here. Otherwise, you're simply an outsider, a commodity to be exploited."

I sat back and laughed. "Now I won't take things so personal."

She stood up and kissed me on the cheek and said, "no, you can't." She gave me her number and told me to call her Thursday evening. "I will set you up with an excellent source in order to get you inside coverage on this story."

I told her that I couldn't thank her enough. She said, "oh you have to make me a promise now."

"Yes, anything. What is it?"

"When the elections are over you must come with me to visit Uganda and see the orphanage that my mother works for." I told Fazia that I would be honored to do such a thing!

That Friday evening after work, we met with her unnamed source at a very private posh French restaurant in the middle of Nairobi. I was overwhelmed with the factual information being poured at me gushing like the rhythm of the Nile. For the sake of privacy and protection, I will simply call this source Charles.

"It's very important, my friend, that foreign journalists like yourself come here. It decreases our sense of isolation. But at the same time, it raises our expectations and hopes. The opposition has learned that there is a shared sense of solidarity with foreigners when it comes to the issue of human rights. I am sure that you've heard all of this before, and it may allow your sense of mistrust and skepticism to grow deeper. Yes, time is needed, patience is needed, but the Kenyan's people's time and patience have run out!"

I took this as a clear omen of the graveness of the changes that may be coming. Two weeks later, on Dec. 30th 2002, Mwai Kibaki won a landslide victory, ending President Daniel Arap Moi's twenty-four-year rule and his KANU's political party's grip on four decades of power.

My article went something like this.

Jubilant crowds in Kenya turned out by the thousands in order to watch the handing over of power and the dawn of a new government. Forty years of domination by President Moi's ruling Kenya African National Union party came to an abrupt end. Mr. Kibaki, the former Vice President to Mr. Moi who left President Moi's government over a decade ago, pledged to begin making economic and political reforms immediately.

"My fellow citizens, I am acquiring a country which has been plundered by years of corruption and mismanagement. We have traveled many miles together," President Moi said mournfully, as some in the crowd badgered him. "We have created much, but there is much more to accomplish." Expectations for the new president could not be greater. Homeless children in rags joined well-dressed professional class people today celebrating in the streets, all optimistic that their lives could somehow be transformed for the better.

In the Shadows of the Ancestors

"I never thought I would live to see this day," said Meredith Nyanga, 53, who stayed up all night in Uhuru Park in order to see the transfer of power up close and personal.

The impetuously organized inaugural attracted many African leaders, including the leaders of Zimbabwe, South Africa, Uganda, and Tanzania. But it was the common folks of Kenya, proud but dignified, who made this triumph theirs. They climbed on roofs for a look at their new president. They bulldozed and elbowed their way past security officers. When the new president arrived, they burst into hysteria that some said equaled the festivals held soon after independence in 1963.

"This is freedom," said Allen Moya, 32, a lawyer. "It's like gaining independence for the second time."

The departing President Moi, 78, was from the old-guard of African leaders who demanded absolute obedience from the citizens. When I arrived, it was still illegal to speak out against him. The new president Kibaki, 70, comes from the same generation as Moi but has a completely different narrative. "I promise not to disappoint you," he said. "I am looking forward to serving you with both humility and appreciativeness." Taking on institutionalized corruption will be his priority, says Kibaki. He also plans to restructure the educational system, lowering the cost of primary school for children. "The era of plutocracy is gone forever," Kibaki said. The details of how to go after past financial crimes still need to be worked out. President Kibaki has talked of creating a reconciliation commission to allow former government officials to admit their past crimes as well as a prosecutorial body to push forward backlogged cases. Today Kibaki said he would not engage in any form of political purging, but would not close a blind eye on the corruption and crimes of the past either.

The president of the IMF, James D. Wolfesohn, said that if President Kibaki begins a serious crackdown on corruption, it could prompt global financial institutions to restart aid to Kenya which has been placed on hold in recent years because of concerns of financial mismanagement in the Moi government.

Something very dramatic and transformative occurred there. I was truly blessed and excited to be able to see a peaceful transition and declaration that democracy can work in a large black African nation, especially a place that had been under the tutelage of overt white supremacy for a long time. South Africa certainly fit that bill.

The next week was a national holiday. With time off work, I took Fazia up on her offer to visit the orphanage in Uganda. We took the 2nd class bus traveling over nine hours down the winding red dirt roads through the Kenyan countryside into the green rolling hills of Uganda. We pulled into the bus station of Kampala; a small, dirty, and overcrowded beehive. Luckily for me, Fazia was very familiar with the landscape and how to maneuver around. We took a taxi through the jammed narrow streets of Kampala, speeding in and out of traffic, going up and down steep hills. The orphanage was on the outskirts of town. It was a small off-white, stoic-looking building surrounded by overgrown weeds and old day mud played in by jubilant children lost in the innocence of youth. In the doorway was a very regal lady with an elegant red dress, hanging gold loop earrings, and classy pepper/white hair. Fazia ran to her warm arms and hugged her like someone who's discovered an oasis in the middle of the desert. Her mother was deeply dignified and gave off an aura of royalty, a person who was very comfortable in her own skin, someone whose compassion overflowed effortlessly into the lives of others. Certainly, the fruit didn't fall far from the tree. That evening, under the pristine, clear, starlit Ugandan night, the children performed local dances, and some of the volunteers shared local folk stories. Among so much poverty and loss, there was a covenant of love that surrounded and infused the entire orphanage. We slept outside that night and watched the stars dance around the low clouds partially covering the surrounding hills. I wondered what cruel turn of fate would have allowed such innocent children to meet such a challenging fate. I looked at them and saw myself and somehow recognized that their challenges were our challenges. We had to make it a matter of life and death. Not many are prepared to go so far. But this resolute single-minded and terrified ruthlessness to help the underdog and pursue the truth masked my obvious vulnerability, my paradoxical and very real helplessness to change the world. There was a young girl, frail and dying of AIDS, yet happy and joyful to be held, happy to be nursed, happy to be loved. Fazia cried and held on to my arm. I breathed deeply and wanted to weep long and loud, to be held in Fazia's arms, to hide my face in her breast, to tell it all, to let it out, and to be reborn in a better world. Was I dreaming? I can't tell. My pride became my mask, both my protection and my affliction. My own fortitude imprisoned me. That day I wished to break my silence and found that I could not express myself. The journalist could no longer be distinguished from his writing.

The next morning, we traveled to the city of Jinja, where the Nile River begins its arduous journey towards Egypt and finally the Mediterranean Sea. We held one another's hands throughout the day and watched the sun set over Lake Victoria. We kissed and held each other that night. We finally revealed our feelings for one another. The sad news is that Fazia had been engaged since she was 14 years old. Her family had arranged this sacred marriage many moons ago.

I asked her, "would you consider ever leaving and coming to the United States with me?" She looked at me for some time silently and then responded, "and break my mother's heart again? Besides you'd have to convert to Islam, and I know you don't like organized religion." Our eyes simultaneously filled with water. We knew then and there that we could never be more than very special friends. At that moment our hearts beat as one!

We had to return to Nairobi the next day. During the bus ride back, I thought about both the highs and lows of this trip, the social changes taking place in Kenya, the heartbreak with Fazia, and the deep changes that had occurred within me. Like the young Maasai warrior on the lonely plains of Kenya, who would have to kill a lion as part of his initiation into manhood. Kenya was my baptism by fire into the stark, wonderful, transformative, sometimes dark realities that are Africa. In the language of the Maasai people I leave you with *ashe oleng*—thank you very much!

Chapter Five

Cape of Storms

"In the Zulu worldview we do not fear death like they do in the western world. We believe in the eternalness of the soul. What dies is the body. The soul is everlasting. Death is simply an obligation of life."
—Zulu saying

South Africa can best be described as a place that has all the best qualities of Africa and many of the worst. I can remember my first flight into J'oburg. It was literally like flying into any Midwestern American town. The homes were developed, the roads were paved, and it was blossoming with modern conveniences.

As I exited the airport and was greeted by my friend Antonia and her family; I was astonished. This was the vision or ideal that I wanted Africa to be! It seemed like a million miles away from the underdevelopment that marred Ethiopia and Tanzania, or the blatant poverty mentality that enveloped Kenya and Uganda.

The first place that my friends took me was to a suburb of Santon. There was a feeling like being in Los Angeles, with its glitzy malls, diverse population, as well as its intensely materialistic vibe. I was amazed at how cheap many things were here in South Africa even in comparison to countries like Kenya and Tanzania.

Later that evening, we went to eat at a game meat restaurant. It was amazing to have crocodile, buffalo, zebra, and even elephant on the menu. My thoughts wondered to how this type of food would repulse many people back in the United States.

That brought me to another observation about South Africa. Its diversity was comparable to the United States. This made me feel right at home, as I thrive on diversity.

Later that evening, we all settled at my friend Antonia's home outside of the all-black suburb of Soweto.

Her home was small but surprisingly spacious. There were great number of guests there when we arrived as this is typical of African homes both large and small. There was always this sense of social interactions pervading African households, and South Africa was no different.

The next cultural nuance that I noticed about South African interaction was the love of what seemed to be pernicious gossip. It began with my friends talking about their jobs and the people involved there. There was a profound individualism within the culture. It reflected in many ways the values of my own American upbringing.

The legacy of apartheid was still fresh as the majority of the neighborhoods were still segregated along racial lines. There seemed to be a tremendous awareness of race within the larger South African society that even surpassed the United States. Amongst the Africans, there are several distinct tribes with the Zulu being the most famous or infamous. Other groups include the Indians, Cape coloreds, coloreds, or the split between the Afrikaans and the British-descended whites. In the midst of the wonderful amalgamation of mixed people, there was still an overwhelming sense of separation and anxiety between different groups.

I felt as if I went back in time, living in the days of Jim Crow in the Southern USA. My associate's families even reflected this deep racial and ethnic divide. Every last one of them were married to someone from their own background and ethnicity. There was surely always tension in the air in this part of Johannesburg. There was always the lingering threat of violent crime buzzing in the ears of everyone. As I spoke with diverse people about the crime issue, it became harder and harder to decipher what was reality and what was hysteria.

The same racial subjugation that I experienced in the United States was even more pronounced in South Africa. There seemed to be a severe lack of consciousness regarding black awareness. Of course there was the deeply embedded memory of Apartheid, yet still, there appeared to be an aloof approach to the remaining plight of other Africans.

The distinction of economic classes was even more pronounced than the racial divisions. Many of the blacks and coloreds came into what is referred to in the United States as "new money." There was an arrogance with the newly wealthy that was hard to stomach.

The level of disrespect that black South Africans gave to other Africans was repulsive. This sickness of self-hatred is what the great writer Frantz Fanon wrote about in his famous book the *Wretched of the Earth*. The deep down self-hatred that plagued so many Africans was magnified in South Africa.

I then made my way down to Cape Town for the week. This unbelievably beautiful town seemed on the surface at least integrated and progressive. An openness seemed to be lacking in Johannesburg. A lack of pretension in many of the open quarters in which I observed. The overall physical outlines of the city were overwhelmingly beautiful and serene.

There was a real sense of serenity and progression in the air. One could feel the sense of opportunity and wonder in the air. The physical beauty of the area was overwhelming. The vibrancy of the people and the diversity of the population was pulsating. The culture was vibrant and diverse. It reminded me of a hybrid between San Francisco and New Orleans. There were a lot of fine international restaurants, cafes, galleries, and upscale bookstores. Different foreign accents and faces lined the street wherever I walked. There was a much more peaceful vibe here in comparison to Johannesburg.

We then made our way down to a town named Frankenhoek where there is a community of French Huguenot wine growers who settled there in the late 1600s. The scenery was spectacular, reminiscent of the majestic Swiss Alps, but in Africa. There was a peaceful and upscale atmosphere, but it was also a little snobby.

That evening, I reminisced on my entire trip in South Africa thus far. I pondered as I wandered what would it have been like to grow up in this country. How would I have benefited from the tremendous sense of transformation that this society has seen? Being born in the majority of any country surely must have a positive psychological effect. This country whose history is very similar to my own, whose diversity is as extensive as my own, and whose racial and social politics are as complicated as our own... what does the future hold here? There was a change in the air everywhere. There was a genuine sense of the sky is the limit and the dawning of a new day.

I took a weekend journey to the remote and sparsely populated country of Namibia. Since my childhood days, I have always been intrigued with this mysterious land of desert elephants and magical horses with unknown origins. The land of wonderful San people, ancient nomadic hunters who played the starring roles in the movie called *The Gods Must Be Crazy.*

There was also the Fish River Canyon, which deeply resembles our own Grand Canyon. I was seriously amazed at the natural fauna and wildlife that were endemic to Namibia.

The capital city of Windhoek reminds one of a small Bavarian city placed in the middle of an African plateau. The actual people were a strange mix of traditional African culture, conservative German traditions, and an unusual blend of South African Afrikaans and Baster culture. Namibia has one of the oldest deserts in the world, and the energy reflects that in the matrix of its unique landscape, cultures, and vibrant history.

I was interested in the most recent history of Swapo, South West Africa People's Organization, and its monumental fight for independence. The old guard of Swapo was still in power and carried a very intriguing story. Swapo, like many other black liberation movements in Africa, has often been overlooked and underestimated. This is particularly the case within the many neo-colonial types of governments which tend to permeate southern Africa. I was walking around the bay area of Swakumound, and I felt a sense of deja vu. It was here that I could almost see yesterday and hear the crying sounds of falling German sailors.

The cuisine of Namibia was extremely diverse, having everything from Portuguese sausage to Angolan beef. Part of the history here in Namibia is transverse with internationalism.

Much of the country's wealth is in the hands of a few German-descended Namibians. This form of economic neo-colonialism was common throughout most of Southern Africa. Unlike other parts of the continent, Europe had possessed this region so completely. And to me even after many years, something of a fantasy remained behind with all the reminders of their presence. Growing up in the West, one might have expected me to be familiar with this type of social stratification. The United States was at least as multi-faceted as Southern Africa. Western culture, as it expressed itself in the United States, was not the same social root of so much that I would experienced in these countries. For in the Africa of my childhood, the land which in my imagination was an extension, alienation was nurtured by the reality of my surroundings. This was more pronounced in South Africa than any other country on the continent.

Since Nelson Mandela stepped down as the president of South Africa in May 1999, much to the contention of those who predicted the worst for a South Africa ruled by the African population, the economy did not collapse and the nation's politics are as dynamic and healthy as they were when the African National Congress (ANC) won the first free elections in 1994. It has failings, and there are certainly many, but they are no greater or more widespread than those occurring in similar countries going through a transition. This country is not only vibrant and progressive; it has passed the most difficult test of political stability—the democratic rite of passage of replacing one leader with another.

Part of the reason for all this was the procedure of Nelson Mandela's departure from office, the way he organized it, the way he began preparing for it almost as soon as he took office. He said from the onset that he would serve no more than one five-year term. It was a brief leadership for a man who had waited a lifetime to lead his people, but he kept his promise, a rare thing for a government official in post-colonial Africa. Like that other old wise man of African politics, the late Julius Nyerere of Tanzania, he gave up the presidency voluntarily, but unlike Nyerere, Mandela did it in a much shorter span of time. In this case, it wasn't even an issue of looking before he leapt. There would have been many in both South Africa as well as abroad, who would have been elated to give him another five years in the halls of Pretoria.

It was my personal experience that Mr. Mandela's voluntary withdrawal from the country's post-Apartheid political stage was an even more significant contribution to South Africa's long-term progress than his histrionic rise into it in the previous decade. It is a tribute to his legacy that the social, political, legal, and civil institutions were as vivacious on the day he left office, as they were when he was sworn in as South Africa's first truly democratically elected president.

The contrast between this new South Africa and the country now inherited by the ANC could not have been more marked. Many conservative whites argue that the entire country has been highjacked, and is being held hostage to a single party. This analysis fails to take into account that there has really been one party domination since the 1950s. This was in many ways hugely different from anything that happened elsewhere on the continent. The vast majority of Africa's post-independence leaders are primarily known for blocking their democratic political processes, not nurturing them.

This seemingly transformative break with the horrible record set elsewhere on the continent led many to assume that Mandela's situation was something ground-breaking, if not revolutionary. Seemingly, almost overnight he became the thing he feared most: the veneration of a personality cult. Superficially, it seems that the cult of personality regarding leaders was commonplace in Africa where presidents had worked hard to ensure that they were the puppet masters of all things. Their touched-up portraits were hung everywhere from train stations to small kiosks. South Africa was a different situation, here the mantle of power had not been appropriated by charismatic command, or bestowed by party dynamics, but was levied on Mandela by public popularity. The admiration was as deep and profound abroad as it was at home, and it began the minute Nelson Mandala walked out of prison after serving twenty-seven years.

Even his most adamant detractors had to admit to a grudging respect for this man who seemed a million miles from the stereotypical corrupt, self-centered, caricature of African leadership the world had come to expect. He was, many argue, a new leader for a new time. People began to refer to the new South Africa as a miracle, and to Mandela as the saint who had made it plausible.

In truth, President Mandela's strategy was not so new, and the destruction of Apartheid was merely the last battle in a protracted long war; a war against white domination and colonialism. South African Apartheid represented the last thorn of the white post-colonial power structure.

President Mandela was not Africa's first political prisoner turned elected official. Many colonial powers, whether the French in Senegal or the Portuguese in Mozambique, had a magic of creating heroes out of the men they had tried to oppress. The African past would suggest that a stint in jail, courtesy of a colonial power, is a prerequisite for future leadership. In 1990, it was prime time for what seemed like history unfolding before our eyes. However, Nelson Mandela was not the first black leader to exit from prison apparently free of bitterness. Both Jomo Kenyatta in 1961 and even Robert Mugabe in 1980 each preached reconciliation after leading bloody anti-colonial uprisings against white rule.

This willingness to overlook and forgive, this deep need for consensus, this core desire for inclusivity is much more than mere political pandering. It is an intricate part of the African psyche, as ancient as the people themselves. For centuries, traditional chiefs have been gathering their communities and trying to find reconciliation and harmony. The search for wholeness and complementariness finds expression in the distinctively African spirit of Ubuntu. It is a very complicated concept to translate directly into English, or for that matter into Western thought. Broadly, it is the notion that one person's humanity is inextricably linked to the cord of humanity in others. The destruction of a former adversary, therefore, has no context in Ubuntu.

On the surface, Africa is littered with hostilities that show little trace of the spirit of Ubuntu. Nigeria, Somalia, and most definitively Rwanda, appeared to prove a more vicious reflection in the communal relations of the continent. The vast majority of these conflicts have been the result of corrupt leaders twisting and perverting ethnic and tribal rivalries for selfish political ends. It very often proves that adversarial politics, especially backed by foreign interest and money, can uproot even the most ancient of Africa's traditions. In modern times, the indigenous community or Tribe, once the equinox of social stability, has often been misrepresented to reflect quite the opposite.

In the so-called democracies of the West, Europe, and North America, old allegiances to clans or tribes are believed to have disappeared long ago to give rise to new loyalties. With the rise of unbridled capitalism, communities began to worry more about which leaders would protect their factories from foreign competitors. Class became paramount over bloodline, as working people in one area became unified with laborers from another completely different geographic area than themselves. In the West, the majority of political parties had to prove above all else that they were savvy organizers of a nation's wealth.

For the majority of Africa, it is not a nation's economic growth that requires protection but rather its ever scarce resources. A very dysfunctional system of loyalty and patronage has become the magic wand to getting a slice of the pie. A very limited shrinking pie at best. When there is not enough, or at least the perception of not being enough, the unspoken rule has been to give first to your tribe or ethnic group. However, for this to happen, you have to be in control. So in many African nations, ethnicity and tribe have been the passport to political and economic power.

Nelson Mandela resisted the seduction of tribal politics, but he was not unique in this. Many African leaders followed this noble path, though many fell by the wayside when their political future was put to the irons.

So President Mandela was not the pioneer of a new order but the last, and perhaps the best of the old. Because of a mixture of outer circumstances, the political environment, and dare I say luck, he was able to progress further than the other leaders, in a shorter time, and with more success. He was what Jomo Kenyatta promised to be, what Samora Machel tried to be, what Patrice Lumumba could have been, and what Julius Nyerere was. He is special because he got it right, not because his approach was new or revolutionary. His leadership marks not a departure from Africa's post-colonial principles, but a reaffirmation of those traditions. If he managed the transition from middle-aged guerilla fighter to elderly statesman more successfully than others, it was partly because the world had transformed so much. Africa had also changed and learned some very trying lessons.

The image of the wise, tall, gray-haired elderly man walking out of the prison gates, fist clenched, with the African sun rising in the background, will forever be etched into the collective human experience. He was a person for all people and cultures. In a world that had become skeptical and fatigued of politicians with empty promises and hypocritical actions, Mandela projected a moral dignity and noble integrity.

When he finally entered into the global area of politics, he didn't disappoint. His true integral leadership shone through on the world stage. Presidents, entertainers, businesspeople, and scientists all rushed to the path that led to his residence. It was as if his dignified moral weight would somehow rub off on them. He would find the deepest respect and reverence worldwide, except perhaps in the banalest recesses of the dark hole of international right-wing politics.

On the home front, he would eventually have to synthesize two roles, loyally defending his disempowered African brethren while at the same time reassuring the white population that a democratic South Africa would be a place where all could prosper. This mediating act between white fear and black need would become the overarching vision of his five-year presidency.

These two seemingly conflicting concerns were not mutually exclusive. Mandela had the foresight to understand that any hope of recovering the economic, social, and even political dignity of the black masses depended, in small measure, on securing that the educated and skilled white population continued to pull the levers of economic expansion.

He needed a unifying vision, something that would bind together these two potentially conflicting goals. He found it in the act of reconciliation. To many black South Africans, this was a call to forgive (but not forget), to resist the temptation to seek revenge, in the interest of greater prosperity, while white people were offered a chance to atone for their past sins. This was the deal implicit in Mandela's policy of reconciliation and nation building.

One of the largest obstacles that South Africa faced was how to handle its painful past. This dark shadow can still be seen and felt within every community today. It lingers like a thousand-pound rock carried by everyone born in this beautiful, yet at times tormented land.

A week later, I was able to travel to the platteland north west of Johannesburg. This area is considered one of the last strongholds of the diehard Afrikaners, the ancestors of those who fled what they saw as the openly liberal Cape in the Great Trek of the 1830s. I was in the heart of the land that gave birth to such extreme right-wing groups as the Conservative Party and the Freedom Front. I was able to interview a Boer farmer named Rian Verwoered. He was tall with a hardened face that was deeply wrinkled from working too many hours in the bright African sun. He had cold blue eyes that underscored a deep sensitivity, as if somewhat warped as well as a nostalgic longing for yesteryear.

With his buttoned up flannel tunic, Mr. Verwoered was quite autocratic at the head of the table, down the center of which ran an arrangement of stuffed Boerewors, and it was at this time that I realized that the farmer had arrived slightly drunk to our lunch interview. He mentioned, unprompted, that he was "observing" the crises of South African democracy with interest. "Ah, Mr. Mandela is an honest man, and he has done well by his African people. He is like an old chief taking care of his tribe." I thought he was building a case for a simple reconciliation within the nation. However, his conversational course; almost a soliloquy—was much broader. "What

keeps a nation together? Not economics. Love. Love and family. That is the
South African way.... You can feed my cat, but she won't obey you. She'll
obey me. Where's the economics in that? That is love and relationships.
Since 1948 we whites have ruled this nation. Power of life and death. I
could have hanged a man and nobody could have done anything to me...
Now they've looted my honor, my privilege. We Afrikaans have become
irrelevant, less important overnight! I often stay up at night, worried
that somebody is going to try to kill my family members or me. Maybe
some black will come and loot away my life's work on this farm. This
isn't about economics; it's love and relationships. You are standing in the
heartland of the Apartheid movement. I ask you where's the cruelty that the
international media talks about? I tell you we are happy in our own part of
this land... Who's needs patriotism? Have no cause to be reconciled about
anything or with anyone. This new government took away everything.
Honor, land, titles, all looted. I will never be a patriot of this new
government, but I am Afrikaans. They must simply leave us to continue our
life here alone. We've had to be cruel in order to maintain some semblance
of civilization in this jungle. We are now governed by sub-humans, and the
world will eventually see this. Are you happy where you come from, Mr.
Hassan? Are they happy in the United States with integration?"

In spite of myself, my anger was rising. I said, "they're very happy in the
United States." He broke out and laughed. However, he had spoken from
the heart. He was a little drunk, but he believed everything he said.

One can only imagine the overwhelming fear that encapsulates all
of South Africa's citizens during these very deep and painful moments
of change and healing. Mr. Mandela and other leaders believed that the
only way to safely navigate through this turbulent, lengthy, divisive, and at

times expensive process was to follow the golden rule of the middle way, a synchronization between retribution and impunity.

The Truth and Reconciliation Commission's guiding principle was to be that very essence of the African humanity. This Commission was made up of a selected group of women and men who would have the unenviable task of shining the torch of truth into the murky depths of South Africa's recent past. Together they would have to find the strength to listen to many Apartheid victims and the forgiveness to grant amnesty to those who were willing to admit their misdemeanors.

For a couple of years, the commission held meetings around the country. Its hearings on human rights violations became platforms where the victims of Apartheid could reclaim their dignity, speaking publicly, often for the first time, about the horrors they had kept locked up in what can be described as, "the well of secrets." There would be no legal precedent; its overriding purpose was to establish the truth so that no one in South Africa and even the world could ever again utter those words of disguised culpability, "we didn't know." It was a noble enterprise to say the least, to actually distinguish between the sin and the sinner, to hate and condemn the sin while being filled with compassion for the sinner.

With the help of a friend, I was able to track down a relative of one of the first witnesses to ever come before the commission; her name was Nohle Mohapi. As it happened that she was now a victim to a social ill that was more modern, yet just as egregious, "Corrective Rape." The irony is that modern South Africa has one of the most progressive constitutions in the world, pledging equality for all of its citizens and protection from all forms of discrimination on the grounds of race, gender, and sexual orientation.

However, the reality is that these high ideals are rarely translated into the everyday interpersonal relations between its citizens.

The so-called Equality Act, passed in 2001, specifically targets "hate crimes," where people are targeted purely because of their identification as part of any specific group. In theory, this includes crimes that target individuals because of their sexual orientation; in practice the vast majority of cases that have been brought to the courts are primarily those based on race and gender. In most parts of the country, there has been a grave failure to implement the promises of the constitution in defense of gays and lesbians. This often leaves gaping holes in an unresponsive criminal justice system that allows many attackers to go free.

I met Nohle at sunset, on an unusually warm winter day in a small shanty home on the border between Soweto and Elderado Park, a former colored township. She was surprisingly outspoken and confident for a victim of such a terrible crime. She said, "every day you feel like there's a time bomb going to explode. You don't have freedom of movement, you don't have personal comfort to do as you please, you're always afraid, and all aspects of your life feel restricted. As women and as lesbians, we have to be very aware that it is a fact of life that we live in peril in many ways.

I met my partner during our teen years, and we became best friends. It was as if we each intuitively knew that we were different from the other girls on our football team.

Zela was confident in who she was. She was an athlete and a very good student. Ambitious and clear of what she wanted out of life. I still find it hard to believe that she could be killed in such a brutal manner. It wasn't the average type of murder where someone simply gets shot or stabbed.

There were rape and humiliation involved. What kind of hatred could those people have had for her when she had done nothing but be herself?

After I found out what happened to her, I went to the area where this terrible act had occurred. When I arrived, her clothes, belongings, and even her blood were everywhere. Even after the police investigation, they just left her belongings there, scattered like the wind. I can never forget the look on her mother's face as she stoically wiped the blood upon her hands and knees.

After experiencing such a brutal and barbaric act, up close and personal, I can't help but feel afraid and unsure all the time. I have been beaten and harassed myself. I live with the tangible threat of rape every day of my existence within the townships. I use to try to resist, to fight back in some way, often on my own and at a great physical disadvantage and personal pa. With time, I realized the futility of struggling on my own and decided to resist in other ways. I am now working with a grassroots organization that is trying to insure the rights of lesbian and gay persons within black and collared communities. We run awareness and education campaigns and even work with local police and government agencies so that homosexuals in our communities can feel comfortable reporting hate crimes."

As I looked deeper into the injustices being committed against lesbians, I realized that Zela's case was unfortunately not unique. There are hundreds of other similar crimes that continue to go unreported and unheard in this budding land over the rainbow.

Has South Africa come full circle? The South Africa that I experienced was not so much a dreamland as a reflection of the globe. Within its borders were to be found great unresolved conflicts between black and white, rich and poor, old and young, and homosexual and heterosexual. There is a new generation that looks back not so much in gratitude as in regret. This new generation was born into a nation under black rule. They understand that what is happening in their country is not what was promised in those intense days when youngsters could only dream of a better tomorrow. They now perceive that the responsibility and power to transform things rest with them in a way that it rested not with the previous generation. They are holding the reins at a time when the world is changing so fast that it is no longer patient enough to wait for Africa to catch up.

Chapter Six

A Land of Pyramids and Slaves

"Africa a continent where throbbed the heartbeat of the world."
—Author Unknown

Fascination, wonder, attraction; it's not easy to identify the source of one's interest. Balad-es-Sudan, The Land of the Blacks, as Sudan was historically known, and has always held mystic wonder for me. Perhaps it's the country's historical and cultural links with Egypt, its on-going political and social tensions, or the decades-long civil war which seems to have finally abated with the formation of the "new" South Sudan. The more tangible issue of government-sponsored genocide in the Western Darfur region was my immediate reason for going.

In the morning, with the smells of dung (waste) fires and wood smoke lingering in the air, a small army mustered to escort the redemption team to where the slaves had been brought during the night. Two dozen soldiers, a few armed only with spears, lined up in front of the bungalow. Drenched in sweat and dust, I felt in need of a shower and also a few more hours sleep. I tried to read myself to sleep with an old Deepak Chopra book on metaphysical principles. When that didn't work, I got out my diary, propped it against my upraised legs, and attempted to visualize a spiritual out of body experience, but it was impossible to settle my mind. Finally, a wave of exhaustion washed into my unconsciousness, but soft thuds above woke me up. I flicked on the light and saw spiders and beetles dropping out of the thatch ceiling onto the mosquito net, crawling down the sides with a scratching of busy legs. A bat darted through the flashlight's beam, quick as an apparition. I lay wide-eyed and cringing until dawn. Two cups of freeze-dried coffee barely cleared my head, but now the scented air and the soldiers standing at attention, and the early light glinting off rifle barrels and spear points quickened my senses.

The walk was a short one down a footpath through the dune grass, past a dried-up water hole ringed by palm trees, a background against which the spear-carrying soldiers made a picturesque sight-click. We came to a small homestead, with a beehive hut where two Arabs waited, sitting on bamboo chairs; the same two I'd seen in the marketplace yesterday—one bearded and the other clean shaven. Both of them were very well dressed: fresh robes and turbans, leather shoes instead of sandals, rings on their fingers, and elegant watches on their wrists. The soldiers fanned out to encircle the homestead and an enormous mahogany tree nearby. There was a bit of conversation, then the bearded one parted the branches and held them aside. I followed them into a shaded circle, and there the slaves huddled in the cool red dust, faces blending with shadows so that all I saw at first were four hundred eyes shining white and lifeless. They were all women and kids, barefoot, and dressed in rags. As my vision adjusted to the dimness, I saw a naked chest ridged with scars, and the absence of pattern told me that they were not the decorative marks with which some Dinka ornamented their bodies. No one spoke, even the babies were silent, lying limp in their mothers' laps, hair reddened and some of their tiny bellies bloated from malnutrition. The only sound was the hum of flies, and the only movement was the flutter of bony hands brushing the flies away. One adolescent boy who did not have a hand, swatted with the puckered stump of his wrist. Another sat with his legs spread-eagle and a crude crutch at his side; he was missing a foot.

As this brutal practice began to manifest itself in the open, I lost all sense of objectivity and journalistic professionalism. I jumped up and yelled out, "these are fucking human beings! People, for Christ's sake!" Everyone there, including the two Arab slave merchants, sat there stoically almost passively. Everyone except me seemed to be devoid of emotion. They continued as if they were making an inventory of inanimate objects. Swaddled in unlaundered clothes, bodies that hadn't known soap and water for weeks or months threw off a dense, sour, salty stench. People, human beings who'd been whipped, who'd had a hand or a foot lopped off because they tried to escape. For the first time in my life, I was confronted with the living stark reality that had enveloped my ancestors hundreds of years ago in a land called America.

To me, the Sudan is more of a region and less a country. It is ethnically diversed and segregated, with black Africans in the south, Arabs in the north, nomadic Bejas in the east, and the scattered Nubians who have a cultural stretch all over the country. Over a hundred languages are spoken, and from several different language families: Hametic, Nilo- Saharan, Semitic, and many diverse tribal tongues. English is the official language of the newly formed South Sudan region.

Acquiring the Sudanese work visa was next to impossible for an American journalist. IRIN news agency had to issue a letter on my behalf; a sort of permission slip, which cost a hefty $100 and which involved a seven day-day procedure where I had to sit in an enclosed glass booth and

slide my documents through a metal tray under the window. The wording
of the letter was that awkward diplomatic-speak, "The Embassy of the
United States would like to take this sincere opportunity to avail itself to
the esteemed Embassy of the Republic of the Sudan, and renew its highest
considerations... etc."

The Sudanese embassy, on the other hand, had a less formal
atmosphere. Inside was like a bustling market with people milling about
from window to window without any thought of queuing or showing
any inch of politeness. Only after my third visit was I given the proper
paperwork to fill out. On the last day, I was instructed to photocopy my
passport, in triplicate, and then come back the next day. On my last visit
to the embassy, the staff had become so familiar with me, I was simply
allowed to roam around inside the offices unattended; strolling from office
to office, where I was served heavily-sugared tea and then left alone while
the workers went off to the prayer room to honor the Muslim oath of
worshiping five times a day. Sometimes the occupants never returned, so I'd
have to stroll another corridor until I found an employee. Eventually, I was
issued the visa for $250.

The air-conditioned train from Cairo to Aswan, in Upper Egypt, was
pleasant. I'd taken Egyptian trains before and always found them efficient
and clean. This was the overnight train which lasted twelve hours. It was
hard to sleep at times as the porter would at times slam open the door and
turn on the light in my compartment for no apparent reason other than
curiosity about the Afro-American traveler.

Aswan is a fascinating city that feels as if it belongs more to African
Sudan than to Arabized Egypt. There are many splendid archaeological
sites, and I believe that here the Nile reaches its foremost elegance. It winds

along the desert route and passes the bewitching Old Cataract Hotel, which plays a prominent role in Agatha's Christie's classic story, *Death on the Nile.*

Aswan is Egypt's third largest city located in the far south of the country. Known in the old days as Swenett, derived from an ancient Egyptian name for trade or marketplace. Because of its location on the southernmost waters of the life-giving Nile, all trading activity was thought to begin and end in this ancient trading post. Small enough to walk around and graced with the most beautiful sunsets on the Nile, the pace of life is relaxing and peaceful. I spent three days there strolling up and down the broad Corniche looking at the sailboats etch the sky with their tall masts. The next morning, I sat for hours at the only Nubian restaurant that I saw in the country. I sat on the balcony listening to Nubian music and eating traditional Nubian cuisine, which both in flavor and texture was in stark contrast to the more Arab food in Cairo. I was just hypnotized by watching the Nile at its most beautiful, flowing through granite rocks and amber deserts, whirling around palm groves and emerald islands covered in tropical vegetation. In the evening, I explored the ancient souk or marketplace. It was full of the scent and color of spices, perfumes, scarves, and baskets.

The marketplace runs along the Corniche, which continues past the Nubian Museum and into a vast cemetery. Just west of the cemetery is the famous gigantic Unfinished Obelisk. Possibly intended as a companion to the Lateran Obelisk, originally placed at Karnak but eventually moved to Rome, if completed they would have been the world's largest piece of stone ever handled.

I stopped off a local café and ordered a dish of curried chicken and rice. The waiter brought me food and handed me a bowl of flatbread along with a plastic pitcher of local citrus juice from a clay cistern. These cisterns are semi-porous, and the leaking juice evaporates as it runs down the sides, resulting in cooling the drink inside. As I began to write down some notes and do some brainstorming, one of the waiters in the café approached me. He was a tall, extremely dark-skinned man with dreadlocks and wearing a loud multi-colored Bob Marley shirt. He introduced himself as Tarik. "I am a native Nubian from a local village named Roku." He spoke broken English with a laid back almost innocent manner. This was in stark contrast to the fast-talking wheeler-dealer types lurking the streets in Cairo. He then whispered in my ear, "do you drink whiskey?" (Alcohol is strongly looked down upon in upper Egypt.) I responded by telling him I preferred to taste the local Nubian wine; a sort of brandy they distil from dates called, *araki Bilah*. This made him smile and burst out laughing. He invited me back to his apartment and opened up a two-liter bottle of local wine, a group of friends in tow.

We drank and talked for hours. Being that I am not a huge drinker, I was happy to discover that the Nubian liquor we drank was considerably sweeter, milder, and smoother than the turpentine-tasting drinks that you find in Cairo. It also lacked the potency. I was then offered the locally-grown cannabis, a rather weak and seed-filled weed they call *bhango*—a sort of small sticky resin wood. A curtain of sweet smoke filled the room. I politely declined a whiff. After the increasing noise level of our partying, Tariq and I went outside to resume our conversation.

"My home village is 70 kilometers down on the border with Lake Nasser. The lake, which was also called Lake Sudan, depending upon which shore you're standing on, was formed after the construction of the Aswan High Dam in the 1960s. The dam not only put an end to the yearly flooding of the Nile in Egypt, but it also forced the migration of my people, sometimes submerging entire villages as well as ancient Nubian historical sites. Most of us left permanently, moving to cities up north such as Alexandria and Cairo, where we face deep racial discrimination from the Arabs. My family is one of the last remaining on our ancestral land."

I couldn't help but to be reminded of the Afro-American's great migration into the northern United States.

The next day, Tariq invited me to a traditional Nubian wedding at a small village located just outside of the center of Aswan. I was initially apprehensive because I had a ferry to catch early the next morning. After pondering over it little more than an hour, I decided that it was a rare opportunity to experience an ancient and rich culture in its most raw expression.

We arrived around 5:30 p.m. as the sun was going down. Upon entering the village, I felt a strange sense of deja vu. It's very hard to explain other than feeling a genuinely heartfelt sense of openness and warmth from everyone. My first and last challenge were obviously the huge language barrier. I was elementary at understanding Arabic, but Nubian is an entirely different world. Tariq, in explaining the nature of his "holy" society to outsiders, would often begin and end by describing the marriage ceremony. Agreements to marry, according to him, may be made while the persons are still infants. Many women are said to marry off children even before they are born! Eventually, of course, the bride and groom must themselves agree to such a union, but rebelliousness towards long-standing family tradition are difficult. I did notice the lack of interaction between men and women during the initial stages of the ceremony. It felt as if everything down to drinking coffee was off limits between the sexes. I asked Tariq what most Nubian men find attractive in a potential spouse? He said, "everything is taken into consideration, not only the girl's appearance, but also her behavior and manner are closely scrutinized. We Nubian men particularly appreciate poise, intellect, and grace in a woman. The bridegroom's family notes carefully the girl's ability to interact and serve visitors with politeness and stoicism."

"If all goes well, the engagement, Firgar, is formalized by a visit to the girl's home by the boy's closest relatives. A meal is served, and the bride-to-be's father announces the reason for the occasion. The oldest or most respected man present asks God's blessing upon the proposed marriage. Following which the entire community recites the first verse, or *sura*, of the Quran. This is often followed up by the reciprocal visit to the groom's house by the bride's family, which helps to facilitate the many detailed arrangements that must be made before the final ceremony."

Afterwards, there was an overwhelming smell of jasmine and frankincense incense everywhere. The music started to play, melodic, intense, yet joyful and upbeat, reminding me of my youthful experiences with the Santeria houses back in New York. The women began to emerge from the houses, and there were gift exchanges everywhere. Personal adornments in gold and silver seemed to signify that she had reached maturity. Gold earrings, ankle bracelets, pendants, and necklaces, the exchanging of henna and hair ornaments were everywhere! Thump! Thump! Thump! The drumbeats were louder, the night sky stars winking and seeming to dance themselves, the lanterns were flickering red in the sand, the brush fires lighted and held up in handfuls to tighten the covering of the huge drums with heat. This was the wedding night, the most important and the climax of the ceremony. Every able-bodied person in the village seemed to move in unison within a circle on the sand. They clapped for the measured line dance, a shuffle back and forth, the circle of men weaving back and forth on the land, singing as they moved. The women danced behind them in groups of five and six, in threes, and fours, their feet and hands locked together at their sides, red and gold striped silk scarves tossed over their black-veiled heads. So measured and controlled was their dance that the loose silk scarves never slipped, but only moved as they moved, to the rhythm of drumbeat and the singing. Gold gleamed in the firelight, with the fine-boned brown faces, the white teeth, and the white drums held high. Thump, thump, thump below the white turbans, the white *gullabiyas*, the brilliant silk scarves floating. The people of the village were dancing. I was dancing on the Nile!

Later that evening, I asked Tariq if he was married or engaged. He mentioned, "I was once engaged to a very beautiful Nubian girl from my village, however after returning from up north for military training, I discovered that she wasn't faithful. If a Nubian bride is found not to be a virgin, no violence takes place, as is often the case in Arab communities. Nubian society takes care of the problem in other ways. Among my community, a paternal cousin must quickly marry a girl who brings this social misfortune upon herself and her family, even if he is already married. The cousin must be someone who will care for the girl and will agree never to mention the reason for their marriage or taunt the girl with her past mistake. This is stated as ideal behavior. Abusing or mistreating the girl in any way is neither expected nor condoned. My heart will forever have a hole in it because of this, but life being like the Nile it is always flowing forward towards the ocean of eternity."

That morning I bought my ticket for the ferry running weekly from Aswan to Wadi Halfa in the Sudan, across Lake Nasser. Booking a first class cabin on the ferry was a good idea, as the rest of the boat was steerage, with people simply sleeping where they could find space: in stairwells, hallways, and even on the bow. I arrived around 8 a.m., and settled into my cabin. I watched the dock from my porthole window. It was total chaos: swarms of people climbing across a barge to enter the ferry, and there appeared to be no limit on luggage. The amount of cargo people brought would shatter any semblance of Western sensibility.

They carried televisions, dragged refrigerators, hoisted tens of cases of canned soda pop. And the baggage… large, over-sized, over-stuffed suitcases wrapped in belts with clothes hanging out. People worked in unison, passing luggage after baggage after boxes over their heads and stuffing anything that would fit into open windows. The police shouted threats and waved batons, but the people simply kept at it, while smiling and singing out that charming word, *malesh*, Arabic for "So what?" or "Who cares?"

Mid-sized vans arrived. Even more people swarmed in increasing heat. Chubby waddling women wearing black hijabs and abayas (headscarves and over-garments) climbed over the trucks to help unload them, while impossibly balancing large parcels on their heads. People passed and carried shrink-wrapped packages of plastic storage containers, washing machines, TVs, large burlap bags of unknown contents. A satellite dish went by, as did ironing boards, and crates of plaster faux-gilded urns. This continued into the evening. The people never seemed to fatigue. They just kept coming.

Later that evening, I decided to stroll around the ship. The hallways and stairwells were packed with passengers dragging luggage and packages around behind them. Up on the deck, makeshift tents constructed out of cardboard boxes and sheets were inhabited by already sleeping passengers. A few young Western travelers were settling in as well, including an innocent-looking Spanish couple who informed me that they were traveling second class. In the dining compartment, where folks playing dominoes and cards occupied most chairs, I met up with a few other foreigners on their way to Sudan: an Italian, a Japanese, and a Dutch woman, all in their early twenties. The Japanese had traveled to Israel and had the misfortune of allowing the Israelis to stamp her passport. The majority of Arab countries don't recognize Israel's right to exist, and they usually don't allow in travelers with an Israeli stamp to enter their country. She simply tore that page out of her passport. The official checking out documents did not notice the missing page.

The Dutch woman was very friendly. She spoke flawless English, and it was hard for me to distinguish if she was American or not. She seemed to have no set agenda or even an organized itinerary for her trip.

We arrived in Sudan without much fanfare. The Wadi Halfa of today seems like an oversized village town. The streets are dusty, and save the occasional mule cart, bizarrely empty. Not surprisingly, none of the banks exchanged money, and only aggressive money-changers in the streets offered the service. I went from bank to bank, just to make sure, but they all confirmed that they had no interest in money changing. The Islamic bank directed me to an obscure and modest looking square which operated a well-stocked exchange.

As I entered the store, a prosperous, tall man with slightly graying hair and a stable, if not noble aura said, "hello, *salaam-alaikum*."

I responded, "Wa—alaikum salaam." I noticed tubs of strawberry jelly and cases of water stacked among the sundries of shaving cream and batteries. We sat and had tea while conducting a small transaction of changing $200 USD in Sudanese pound for a rate of 6.09 to one US dollar.

I had a couple of hours until the weekly train to Khartoum arrived, so I needed to start heading towards the station. A donkey cart driver gave me a lift to the nearby train stop, where I bought my ticket. I requested a first class ticket in the sleeper car, but they were already sold out. I pleaded with the official, and even offered a subtle bribe. This was all to no avail. The official at the Wadi station offered me a second class ticket on the train and assured me that there was no salient difference in comfort he assured me, only price—a few thousand dinars, which was only a matter of dollars. First class cabins seat six and second, eight. Third class was absolutely out of the question; it was tantamount to traveling in a boxcar!!

In the Wadi train station, women had set-up small coffee and tea stands, some of them made from simply salvaged steel boxes and wooden crates. Again like Aswan, there was a crazy amount of baggage piled up all over the dirt platforms. Children climbed over it while playing. A little boy, a toddler, was standing next to his mother's coffee stand. He smiled, and I waved hello, and I smiled back. He did a little dance of happiness, and then ran over to me, unzipped his pants, and then pissed in the dirt next to me. Then he ran off smiling and dancing as he left.

The train arrived about 6 p.m., early May directly on the Tropic of Cancer, the sun was still strong, but the heat was somewhat waning. I boarded the train, placed my luggage on the rack above me, and placed my backpack under my seat. I was the first person in the compartment, so I took a window seat facing the forward direction. People began running wild in the aisles of the train cars, carrying overweight luggage and bags packed full. A heavy-set Arab-looking man shot into my compartment, shook my hand with a huge smile, and then began stacking cases of canned goods in the middle of the floor. For a short while, he actually tried to fill the space under the seats, but he ran out of room and just kept piling them up.

The train ride to Khartoum was an estimated thirty-six hours. The train, a relic from the colonial times, remained in the station for hours. I brought ten liters of bottled water with me. I was really concerned about dehydration and hadn't known how many regular stops were to be expected on the trip to Khartoum. When I say the train left the station, it did so gradually; it crept out of the station, with all the well-wishers waving good-bye from the dusty platform.

The slow pace of the train never seemed to increase. We lumbered, creaked, inched ever onward, and barely at the speed of somebody jogging. In fact, more than one person, huffing and puffing, caught up with and boarded the train hours after it had left the station. The other passengers happily chipped in, along with the porters to help the late-comers get their bags and boxes onto the train, through open doors and windows. Some belongings came haphazardly flying through the windows, tossed from horse-cars galloping alongside the rickety old train, the drivers beating the animals with sticks.

My first week in the Sudan, I easily became fatigued after the sun went down. Of course, the process of traveling lends itself to fatigue. My cell phone was useless in the Sudan, as I'd need a new SIM card for it, so

I shut it off. The phone's clock had been my watch, so I had no idea what time it was as I drifted in and out of sleep during the night, with the cool night air blowing through the open window. The other passengers in my compartment were snoring away, while seated in the upright position, or slumped against each other.

As I awoke, the sun was up, and I asked the guy next to me what time it was. He told me, "Six a.m.," in broken English with a very strong Arabic accent. The air coming through the window was still pleasantly cool, the expansive desert scenery was dramatic in its sparseness, its pure emptiness. I was going to be on this train for another thirty hours, so I stood, stretched, and excused myself from the cabin. I clambered over the people sleeping in the aisle and made my way to the next car, which so happened, was the dining car. It too had been used for sleeping, as there were people slumped all over the tables and chairs. I found an open area and sat down while I made cursory notes on my trip. A uniformed man took my order: tea with a roll and a small packet of crackers. The attendant poured water into the tea kettle, looked as though it'd been drawn from the raw waters of the Nile River, a sort of muddy-brown colored liquid.

I sat down next to a man named Jamal. He had a tranquil and calm aura. He asked, "where is your final destination?"

I answered, "the Darfur region." I then asked him, "do you believe there is a crisis in the Darfur region?"

"No," he assured me. "This is all manufactured. You see, George Bush tried to get into Sudan to get oil."

I responded, "so all the news, photos, and information… Al-Jazeera, BBC, and CNN are making up images of refugee camps?"

"Those images they show are twenty-years old. You can manipulate images very easily when you have an agenda."

"But what about the African Union, the UNHCR, and all the NGOs? Are they also part of some vast conspiracy to get oil out of the Sudan?"

"Hassan, you have to go and see these things for yourself, never believe the news." This seemed to be another dead end conversation. I said, "well, I suppose that's why I am going into the Darfur region, in order to cover the news myself."

No, at this point I didn't have the secret answer to Sudan's complicated and multilayered problems. The fact of the matter was, I'd been on this creeping train for thirty-six hours, and we were only half-way to Khartoum. I wondered why I took this assignment. I would ponder for hours and then slowly lumber off again. One side of the tracks were the green, lush irrigated banks of the Nile, with sugar cane and date palm farms. On the other side of the tracks was the expansive loneliness of the reddish desert rising out of black granite mountains.

The small villages we passed were more frequent, due to the proximity of the Nile for irrigation. Again, small children came scampering out of their mud-brick compounds to wave at the passing train. There was the occasional lone concrete structure, usually a small mosque or prayer house. We followed the ancient trading routes of the Sahara, past the purplish rolling hills on our way south to Khartoum.

When we arrived at the small town of Albaka, I had been on the train for almost forty-five hours, and I have had enough. The train was going to be sitting in Albaka for "about two hours," though no reason was given. From there I could take an air conditioned bus to Khartoum on a semi-paved highway, and the trip was a mere four hours. There was no alternative. I jumped a rickshaw into town and found the bus station. "There's one leaving in thirty minutes? Great, I'll take it." I raced back to the train station to pick up my bags and returned to the bus.

As I entered the bus, the people inside politely tried not to stare, they all looked fresh and were dressed in clean bright white robes. People started sneezing from the dust and burlap fibers that floated off me as I passed them. I sat down and enjoyed my first cool air in many days as the bus pulled off.

As we drove the smooth highway, I watched the desert pass in the comfort of a new bus. After about a half an hour, we passed what according to my map, were the Meroe pyramids (ancient Nubian Kingdom—many tombs go back to the 8th century BC, maybe earlier.) It was hard to be certain in the beginning because from a distance they just looked like symmetrical outcroppings from my view. The Sudan, unlike Egypt, does not make an effort to exploit their ancient ruins for tourism. Essentially, if one wants to tour them, one must apply for a permit and provide or arrange transportation. Acquiring these permits in the Sudan is a long and tedious process.

Farther down the highway to Khartoum lay the city of Shendi. Shendi was once the slave trade capital of Islamic Africa. Thousands of people each year, captured in the lucrative slave raids, were sold in markets in this dusty town and then sent off to the Arabian peninsula and other points in the Middle East. Night was falling, and I finally fell asleep for a short while.

I woke early and realized that the bus was pulling into downtown Khartoum. The mid-day heat was burdensome. After changing money at one of the banks, I immediately tried the telephone number of a fellow IRIN news journalist named John. He was my contact and transportation to travel into the Darfur region. During this time, only NGO's, the UN, and news organizations like mine made trips to the Darfur region. Though he had never met me, he was pleasant and offered to help me book my flight. He agreed to meet me the next day in the lobby of the Mercure Hotel lobby.

The name Khartoum means "elephant trunk." In this place, the Blue Nile, which flows from the highlands of Ethiopia's Lake Tanta, and the White Nile, which flows from Lake Victoria in Uganda, meet to form the confluence which flows throughout northern Sudan and Egypt and finally empties her tears in the romantic Mediterranean Sea.

The next day, I met up with James and he told me that my paperwork was finished and that there were some contacts that he wanted to put me in touch with in Darfur. The police officers at the airport were immediately suspicious of me and asked to see my paperwork. I gently smiled and assured them that all was in order. This seemed to take forever, as each official took turns inspecting my documents. They couldn't quite grasp that I was an English-speaking Afro-American journalist. The flight to Darfur was smooth, calm, and uneventful; a first while traveling in Sudan.

Northern Darfur is a forbidding place. It has landscapes of elemental simplicity; vast sandy plains, jutting mountains, and jagged ridges. A village, sometimes comprising no more than a cluster of huts made from straw and branches, may be a day's ride from its neighbor. Every place, however humble, counts. A hand-dug well in a dry river bed can be the difference between life and death.

The people in this region are resourceful and resilient. Extracting a living from this land requires unrelenting hard work and detailed knowledge of every crevice from which food or livelihood can be scratched. A woman living on the desert edge will know how to gather a dozen varieties of wild grasses and berries to supplement a meager diet of cultivated millet and vegetables, along with goat and camel's milk. She will know the farms and village markets within a hundred miles or more, and will not hesitate to walk or ride such distances to buy, sell, or work.

Darfur is home to about six million people. There is just one rainy season, lasting approximately from June to September, which brings occasional storms to the dry north and steady showers across the much more lush south.

In the center of Darfur, the extinct volcano of Jebel Marra rises 8,000 feet above the surrounding savanna. This verdant mountain can be climbed in a day, an arduous trek through orchards, thorns, and rugged cliffs that extend nearly to the edge of the crater. There are many fabulous myths about the fertility of the rich dark earth found on its crater floor and the mysterious creatures that haunt the deep waters of this crater lake. For many Darfurians, this mountain possesses a mystical quality.

Darfurians, like most Africans, were comfortable with multiple identities. In the 1800s, this area was the most powerful state within the borders of modern-day Sudan. In adopting Islam as the official state religion, the Darfur rulers also embraced Arabic as a language of religious faith, scholarship, and law. Both Arabic and African Fur were spoken of at court. Darfur was an African kingdom that embraced Arabs as valued equals.

It was still hard for me to understand how such deep ethnic and racial divisions evolved in such a seemingly tolerant land. There is a saying here in Darfur, "conflict defines origins." I wondered if this was because people would instinctively cling to their ancestral roots in times of insecurity? Or was it because tribes settled all compensation with blood money!

All Darfurians are Muslims, so this conflict cannot be deduced to a religious one. This fact is due to the historic trade routes that allowed Islam to spread in a peaceful way. Darfur today is defined by ubiquitous abuse and human suffering. There were more than two million people displaced, and another 200,000 were refugees. Hundreds of villages were destroyed. Although death rates have declined since the mid-2000s, the vast majority of the population still lives from day to day in a terrible survival mode. I have observed firsthand the legendary Darfurian resilience.

My mind was still vexed as to how this could happen, and more importantly, why did this happen? I did notice that black villagers in Eastern and Central Sudan often complained that commercial farmers armed with land deeds and contracts confiscated their land. Darfur being so far removed from any profitable markets, there were absolutely no investments from the Sudanese government. The only opportunity for black African Darfurians seemed to be as migrant workers finding employment on irrigated farms along the Nile. Another observation that I quickly assessed was that any cultural exchange appeared to bring about the abandonment of African culture, notably ethnic dancing, drinking traditional beer, the barter concept, traditional African ways of dressing, and the independent status of women. All this has been replaced by a new sense of conformity which includes speaking Arabic, wearing northern Islamic clothing, jellabiya for men and tub for women, shunning alcohol, only using cash, and restricting the role of women in the public sphere.

Ironically, most of the officials that I spoke with all referred this process as one of Sudanization, while the African villagers named it Arabization.

This conversion of Arabization usually occurs in subtle ways; the government often uses schoolteachers, traders, and radical Imams bent on saving the souls of their heathen African brothers. The passionate extremism of their sermonizing and its innate hostility to the more tolerant indigenous and Sufi practices of Darfur's ancestral religious order is captured in the language of the preacher who denounces those as hypocrites those who simply use a plastic or Western toothbrush as opposed to the seven types of twigs claimed to be sanctioned by Islam. The vast majority of Africans in the marketplace tend to wash out the rhetoric by simply turning up cassette recorded music to drown it out. The village chief told me that a well-known alcoholic gave up drinking for a week, missing the companionship of his un-Arabized drinking companions too much. Black African farmers simply could not afford to cultivate without the extra labor of their female family members.

In this village, thousands of people from the Republic of Chad mingle with local Darfurians. Many of them also mixed race between Northern Arabs and Southern Black Africans. During the '90s, the primary complaint was not that the process of "becoming Sudanese" denied them their own individualized cultural expressions, but that the government in Khartoum was not treating them as full citizens of the state. The vast majority of Darfur's towns and villages scarcely have better services than in the days of British colonialism. "We are surviving here only by the grace of God and diesel trucks," stated Sheihk Malik. These large diesel trucks bring the village fuel, food, and other supplies. Sheikh Malik stated that, "so-called Western economic sanctions against the country are raising the price of fuel, sugar, and even tea. Even diesel is being rationed, pushing Darfurians one step closer to total disaster. Darfur is a backwater; a prisoner of geography."

Twilight was a brief intermission between night and day in Africa. The stars twinkled sharp and lucid in the moonless sky. As tomorrow was my first day to interview the African ex-slaves, I couldn't sleep. I searched the sky looking for the Big Dipper. It was there, but like most things in Africa, hidden and waiting to be discovered over and over again. The star seemed to be much closer to the horizon than it was back in the states. Soon crickets, along with the distant roll of a drum call, filled the evening silence. They seemed to make one unbroken chorus, fast and rhythmic, merged into a unit as harmonious as a symphony; Sudan's natural orchestra, and it was playing just for me. I said out loud, "this is happiness, to be dissolved into something greater than ourselves." Oh, this transcendent ideal that I'd sought hadn't brought that elusive spiritual rebirth that I so desperately hunted. Had I discovered it here? Some strange part of me wished that I could remain. In this conflicted, immense, and mysterious country could I begin to see my life anew?

In the morning, with the smells of burning palm chips and dung fires penetrating the air, a small security team assembled to escort us to where the slaves had been brought during the night. The walk was long down a dried out river bank. We came to a cream-colored building; colorless, gray, and foreboding. It resembled an outgrown homestead, built in the middle of nowhere.

"My name is Osman Assam. I am 20 years old. I was captured three years ago. The Arabs attacked my village early one evening."

I sat there behind my laptop, somewhat stunned, and almost unable to look at him. It was midday now, and the sun was shining so strongly that it resembled a giant isolated orange.

I then asked Osman to resume his story. "They came on horseback, many of them. Some wore drab brown uniforms; others wore bright white jellabiyas. They came two on a horse, one to guide the horse, the other to shoot. They shot old people and men. My father was running away, but he didn't make it very far. The Arabs rode horses and were extremely swift. My father tried to defend us with an old wooden fighting stick and shield. The bullets went through his shield, hitting him in the chest and instantly killed him in front of us. I wanted to run, but they would shoot anyone that moved. When they caught me, they tied me to ten other men. I was separated from my wife and son and haven't seen them since." My interpreter Abdul looked at me with one of his hard-to-read stares. We each thanked Osman as he rose and walked outside the interview room to stand with the others. They were all lined up behind the U.N.H.C.R.-marked truck. UN workers were pouring water into tin cans and giving each person a drink. Still stunted by the disturbing stories of murder, rape, and forced labor, I stood up to go to the restroom to wash my face and get my emotional center back.

A twenty- two-year-old woman, Malika Abed said, "and because I would not allow my genitals to be cut, Tariq's sister called me *jengei* (nigger) and filthy infidel. Later that evening, I was told to fetch water from the well. While bending over to fill the cup, I was suddenly struck on the back of the head and knocked down. Tariq and his brother then stripped me naked. They told me what would happen to non-Muslim women with uncut genitals. They proceeded to rape me in a humiliating and painful manner." There was an uncomfortable pause from both Malika and my interpreter! She then suddenly continued, this time with fire in her voice and eyes, "I wish I was a man so I could learn to use a gun. I would kill Tariq and his brother, in fact, I would massacre the entire family!"

Ironically, there was a dark kind of relief, a twisted beauty in hearing this woman's longing for revenge. It was actually a breath of fresh air, after hearing dozens of other ex-slaves recite the horrors they'd suffered from such stoicism. "I would massacre the entire family."

How naïve I'd been to think that I had reached these people with my blind idealism, that somehow my words had given life to their restricted happiness. The chasm between them and I was much greater than the one between Afro-America and Sub-Saharan Africa, between the north and south. They had suffered terribly; I had not. It deeply disturbed me to feel so isolated, so distant from them, the women most of all. I gazed at the barbed wired fence that surrounded the compound and wanted to cry out to the world, "how can people be so cruel to one another?" It hits suddenly and overwhelmingly, like an evil that screams to be destroyed.

The international community's response to the crimes that have been committed in Sudan has often been too little, too late. Many of the human rights abuses that have been reported to the International Court of Justice only target individual perpetrators of these crimes. Racial and religious intolerance will defile the political, social, and economic landscape and the *janjawiid* still gallivant free.

Despite the savagery of the past, many Darfurians still hope to reconnect with their homeland. The task is overwhelming and treacherous. A sustainable peace in Darfur will require more than the previous short-term urgency responses. It needs massive economic and social investments. This, coupled with some semblance of the rule of law, just may allow the people of Darfur to live a decent life and find their proper place within the Nation of Sudan.

Chapter Seven

The Doors of No Return

"The River that doesn't know its source soon dries up."
—Ewe proverb

From afar, the fortress has a clean, almost pristine look. As one moves closer, the ancient castle begins to whisper its dark secrets. Here thousands of African women, men, and children were assembled by force to be shipped off on the notorious Middle Passage voyage. Hundreds of people chained and shackled into tiny spaces awaiting an unknown fate. Inside the fortress were maps showing the most efficient and economical way to load the human cargo onto the ships. Despite the intense heat, I felt cold chills run up my spine, almost as if the ghosts of yesterday were directly here in my presence, and in many ways they were.

Although originally constructed by the Portuguese, Elmina Slave Castle remained a testament to the dark Dutch presence in West Africa. The sense of damage, which the trade inflicted on Africa is on open display here. Wreaths of flowers and bright clothes, empty bottles, and half-burnt candles mark an indigenous spiritual shrine at the bottom of the steps which once led to a forty-yard tunnel into the black waters of the Atlantic Ocean. Looming in the background are four gigantic chambers, dimly lit by hollow shafts of natural sunlight peering through rustic crevices cut into the stone walls. The incessant splashing of the waves and the distant voices of half-naked Ghanaian fishermen scampering in the surf suddenly made it difficult to imagine the savagery that occurred in these dark chambers. Even the chamber floor seems at first to relay nothing unusual, only tightly packed stale smelling dirt one would expect to find in such old enclosures. But in these floors are the remains of lost spirits crying out for redemption, for hope, and for acknowledgment. Pounds of ancient human excrement covered the deepest recesses of the dungeons at Elmina Castle. This was the product of thousands of slaves a year who abided in the dungeons until they said their invocations at the sanctum and walked down the tunnel to European ships waiting to ferry them to the Americas. There were no restrooms.

Our tour guide stated, "this was an experiment. If you could survive down there for nine to twelve weeks, then you were tough enough to be a slave! The dead bodies were brought up and thrown over the enclosure into the ocean."

Elmina Castle is one out of the dozens of fortresses down the west coast of Africa built by dominant European colonial powers from the sixteenth to seventeenth centuries to facilitate trade, much of it for material goods, but the vast majority of it human. From the bend in the Niger River to Namibia in Southern Africa, a distance of 1,450 miles, three and half centuries of enslaving took at least 9 million, perhaps as many as 21 million, enslaved Africans to the new world. The best estimates are that an equal number of people died during the trek to the sea and in raids by other African groups to capture slaves. Perhaps another 3 million more people perished on the journey across the Atlantic when for months, hundreds of slaves on board ship were forced to lie with their faces between each other's legs within a couple of feet between the wooden plank deck and the upper interior of the ship. This trade represented a massive assault on Sub-Saharan Africa's population, which by the time the slave raids ended, was estimated to total between 40 to 60 million people. On the almanac of atrocities executed on the human race, the Atlantic Slave trade rates among the most horrendous.

It was here that gold, for which modern Ghana earned its colonial name the Gold Coast, was the most significant attraction to Africa for the Dutch, Portuguese, French, and the English who arrived on West Africa's shores.

With the birth of the colonies in the Americas came an insatiable need for labor. Millions of indigenous American Indians had already began to be wiped out by European diseases, forced labor, as well as brutal violence. Indentured servants from Europe could not perform all of the work. The West then turned to Africa and its pool of proven black farmers and labors.

Financial gains from plantations in the Americas provided the money England and other countries in Europe needed to jump-start the eventual change from feudalism to capitalism. And so the women, men, and children who walked in chains down the underground passage of Elmina Castle and the numerous others along the coast of West Africa to the awaiting ships, became unwilling accomplices in Europe's Industrial Revolution.

Evening was closely approaching, so I wanted to get back to my hotel. It was huge, pretentious, expensive, yet lacking in sophistication and simple elegance. It's a very well-known western hotel chain that sits like a staid tree in the middle of dynamic African chaos.

After resting a few hours in my room, I was overcome with a strong feeling of anxiety and restlessness. Unable to sleep, I went downstairs to the bar. It was fairly mellow with faint reddish leather seats, a slow groove of Marvin Gaye playing softly in the background. Across from me sat an average looking honey-colored woman. She was speaking angrily on the phone. I waited for her to finish the conversation before making eye contact. We both looked at each another a little longer than is normally expected of strangers. She smiled slightly and extended her hand introducing herself as Carolina. I was a little shocked that an African woman would be so forward!

"Hello my name is Carolina, and you are who?"

I answered, "my name is Hassan how are you?"

"That accent you have, are you from the States?"

"Very good, either you travel a lot or you've lived abroad yourself."

"Yes, I was born in the Ivory Coast, but raised in France."

I offered to buy her a drink, which she accepted; a White Russian. "Carolina, you seem very stressed out. I don't mean to impede into your personal business, but it's simply an observation."

She let out a deep heartfelt laugh. "No offense taken. I work for a major Petro company, so this stress is very normal for me. I am curious to know, Mr. Hassan, why does a black man from the West end up with an Islamic name such as yours?"

"It's a really long drawn out story, and I have much more interesting questions to ask you about Ghana!"

"Okay, shoot."

"Well, first of all, how did you end up moving to France if you were born in West Africa?"

"Well that's simple enough, my father is French, and my mother is originally Cameroonian. They met in the Ivory Coast while he was working on a ship-building project and she was there looking for a job. That was many years ago," she mentioned with a twist of irony.

"What brings you back to Ghana?"

"Work, they have discovered oil reserves off the coast, and our company wants a first leg into the speculation."

"How European of them!"

"Oh don't be so sardonic. Believe me, if Africans weren't getting anything out of it, they wouldn't allow them to set up here."

"Okay, good point."

"Now what are your real questions about Ghana?"

"Actually, I am very much interested in visiting the slave castles." "Being a black American that doesn't surprise me in the least. Did you have a specific slave fort in mind?"

"Well everyone is familiar with the two most popular forts, Elmina and Cape Coast. I was hoping that you could actually recommend someplace less known, more exotic, out of the beaten path."

"Well, my American brother with the Arabic name, look no further for your adventure tour. There is a very beautiful town and fort named Ada."

I put up my hand, as if I was shocked or offended by her last comment. She looked up as if she wanted to apologize for her previous statement, but without knowing why. I smiled and asked her to repeat the name nice and slowly.

"Fort Ada."

"Can you believe that is my mother's name?"

We each burst out laughing. "Really? How fortuitous, you must visit."

We talked half the night about everything from the metros in Paris to the crime in Nairobi. She gave me a tour guide contact that she said was a trusted family friend by the name of Earnest. She said that he would be more than happy to give me a decent price to visit this mysterious fort in Eastern part of Ghana.

The next day, I finally gave Earnest a call to both introduce myself and set up a ride to Fort Ada. We agreed to meet the next day at 6 a.m. He mentioned that it was a three to four hour drive and it would be better if we left early.

Earnest arrived an hour and half late, "But this was pretty good for West African time!" He pulled up in an old gray and white Toyota truck. From the outside, it looked sturdy and well-conditioned and I had a brief sense of relief. Five minutes after sitting in the front seat, I quickly realized that there was no air conditioning in the car. As we pulled onto the main highway with the windows down there was natural ventilation as the wind gently caressed my face. After two hours, we passed the muddy and sleepy town of Tema, continuing through the highway pavement which passed timelessly through red blood-colored dirt and chickens running wild around makeshift kiosks. We heard the sounds of stray dogs barking and the gentle laughter of chocolate colored children innocently blinded from the harsh realities of African poverty.

Shortly afterwards, we reached the somewhat picturesque town of Ada Fort. I was in awe and actually a little tickled that an African town would share my mother's name. Earnest asked , "what would you like to see first?" I told him the local cemetery. We drove for fifteen more minutes until we arrived in front of a run-down old Presbyterian church with an old cemetery in the back. The vast majority of the tombs were of obscure Europeans who had passed away during the colonial times. The graves were old, dilapidated, and strangled by wild vegetation that seemed to want to return them back into the earth. Stray dogs roamed the area, boldly jumping on raised wooden planks and looked out over the cemetery as if they owned it. I was a little disappointed by not discouraged. "I have come to the see the magnificent fort here in Ada."

Earnest told me that the beach was only a short walk away from the Church.

We arrived at a white beach lined with beautiful palm trees, a small wooden walkway, and stalls selling everything from deodorant to used car parts. I stared down the beach in every direction hoping to find the large Castle Kongenstein, a slave fort built by the Danish in the 1700s, I turned around and asked my guide, Earnest, "why I am unable to see any Fort?" He smiled shyly and then pronounced, "the Fort has lost its centuries-old battle with the sea and had hence been swallowed up many years ago. What remains here is a plaque that honors those ancestors who left these shores in chains." He quickly observed my disappointment and wanted to make amends. "My friend, I have a cousin who owns a small boat that makes voyages up the Volta River." This is the most famous river in Ghana and has a plethora of historical significance.

I was happy to be experiencing history on the water. Making our way through the narrow riverbanks, the water was somewhat shallow, so Ernest's friend, a boatman named Nshani, stopped his traditional paddling and began moving the boat by using a long pole which pushed off from the bottom of the river. Moving at a slow pace, time seemed to stand still, passing many small villages, watching fisherman methodically setting their nets, and the sounds of exotic birds singing ancient tunes. The boat suddenly took a sharp left turn, heading towards the Gulf of Guinea finally reaching the mysterious Volta River delta. A swamp-like opening where several dugout canoes were docked. We passed fishing boats with names like Mother Forgive Them, Psalm 25, and Obama painted in colorful, almost loud tones. Yet there was a haunting nostalgia in the air. There is an almost tangible sense of melancholy that pervades the atmosphere. The footsteps of hundreds of enslaved Africans being marched up and down these hidden waterways certainly left an impression that I will never forget. Most of their stories are forever hidden in a treasure box of pain, humiliation, but also redemption and rebirth. This was certainly a land of *sankafo*, a Ghanaian word which means go back and get it.

Looking at the other side of the beach, I could see several upscale resorts and huge multimillion-dollar homes. "That this the playground of Ghana's elite, government ministers, as well as businessman and retired sportsman," stated Earnest. I wasn't really interested in knowing more about it; the economic disparity in Africa is evident everywhere. Being close to the shoreline allowed me to silently ponder about this place named Ada Fort. Enjoying the story told by the silent powerful force of nature, listening to the intense yet soothing roar of thunderous waves pounding the sandy beach allowed me to briefly look back in time and ponder the awesome voyage that my ancestors survived. It was time to say goodbye and leave my mother's namesake in Africa.

Back in Accra, I met with Beatrice Mensah, a forty-year-old founding member of a Ghanaian non-governmental organization called HOPE. Her's is a vision to ensure the sustainability of Ghana's primary resource; its cultural continuity and wisdom of its elders. She believes that many elderly people are being marginalized in Ghana's rush for technological and economic development. "Tradition mandates that we take care of our elderly. But many of these people simply aren't looking at the problem truthfully. The horrific plight of the elderly can be observed across sprawling cities throughout Africa. What would have been unimaginable over a decade ago has become a stark reality in today's world. For hundreds of years, advanced age was regarded in traditional spiritual systems as a blessing, and the elderly were honored as keepers of hidden knowledge, cultural custodians, revered as venerated, the essential connection between the ancestors and the living. In many West African languages, the meaning for the word elder is, *they who know or she or he who sees.* In many parts of Africa, one is simply not considered fully developed until they spend an extended amount of time with their grandparents to learn the wisdom and knowledge that only experience can teach."

I said, "well, I've always heard about this concept back home, but what are the actual details of this deeply ingrained concept?"

Mrs. Mensah replied, "three core principles are the foundation of this law; family unity, communal reciprocity, and social recollection. To neglect one's elders was to commit an inexcusable act of ungratefulness, and the Western practice of placing one's parents in nursing homes was considered heinous, even primitive. There was, of course, sound logic for the ethical stand. If children are considerate of their parents and others in the expanded family, then they too in return would be cared for by their offspring and relatives. Ghana designed a privatized social communal system and positioned it where it would be the most efficient and most effective; within the extended family structure."

I mentioned that in my opinion, there were a lot more dangerous obstacles hindering Africa's growth and progress than just the neglect of their elderly. Things such as AIDS, civil war, nepotism, and unabashed corruption. Mrs. Mensah's voice increased and her argument became more ebullient and fervent. "My dear friend, with the population growth rate slowing and health care improving, the percentage of old people in Africa is expected to increase rapidly in the near future. Even countries hit hardest by the AIDS epidemic, which Ghana isn't included, the elderly have had to redirect the years and reassume their role as head of households, as their children have fallen to the virus and left their grandchildren as orphans."

"Well, who do you blame for this radical level of deterioration of the family unit in Ghana," I asked?

"Much of the fault has to do with Ghana's integration into an egregiously predatory capitalist system! What years of colonialism and even the slave trade had failed to do, break the structure of the extended family, is being accomplished in a very short time by the onset of full-fledged western consumerism. The extended family is the backbone of Ghana's lasting humanity. The resulting economic strains of competing in a global economy have forced nuclear families to look after themselves first, and to think about their communal families second, if at all."

She continued. "I truly believe that in the West, you have lost even the very notion of the extended family. Your culture's intransigent and insatiable need for selfish individualism is partly to blame. Without the extended family, Ghana would have economically and socially plummeted years ago. In many other African countries, kinfolks are the last line of defense against the wave of orphans caused by civil war, famine, and AIDS. I would like to show you this problem Mr. Ansah, up close and personal." Just a few miles from Mrs. Mensah's office in Nima, a suburb of Accra, this process was slowly unfolding.

An active forty-year-old HOPE volunteer named Adika Danso stands unsteadily outside a flimsy tin shanty, taking a moment from her morning chores to gaze at the ceaseless bustle of the Ghanaian capital, Accra, as if she was looking directly into the future. The scene for her is a baffling one; groups of young street hawkers wearing tennis shoes and American styled baseball caps, selling everything from cheap coffee mixes to used auto parts, dilapidated buses squeezed full of passengers careening around one corner, and a massive traffic jam spewing out exhaust fumes.

Adika says that more than anything else, what she and her colleagues are trying to do is act as a surrogate for the communal family. "We visit the seniors in their homes, we pray for them, we sing for them, we listen to them. Sometimes we clean their rooms, brush their hair, wash their clothes, anything to make their lives more comfortable. It's a strenuous duty because you must be patient if they are aged. They can be a bit difficult. That is one of the reasons that many young couples are no longer prepared to live under the roof with the extended family. Another is that the young, often more culturally in tune with their peers in Paris or New York, no longer have patience for their elder's traditional upcountry beliefs."

Adika said, "the poor care of the elderly people in Ghana is something that has come about as a result of the poor economic situation of the people. Old values are changing because of modernization, education, migration, and industrialization. Because of education, we are getting newer skills and new forms of employment. People are moving as a result of education they have received to other areas of work, migrating to urban centers, and leaving behind family members."

I asked the volunteer, Adika, "what do you think the long term solution is?"

"A return to the basics. Simply put, if you have children and look after them, it is a must that they have to take care of you," she says. "Parents should bring forth two or three children, and care for them properly. Then in the future, they can take care of you."

Mrs. Mensah takes a longer view. "The wheels have turned, and there is no turning back," she says. "We can still support family members to look after their elderly because so many people are emotionally attached, people feel guilty that they are not able to look after their elderly. The solution is that young people in countries like ours should begin to look straight into the eye of the aging with a sense of planning. Life has changed, and there is no point in saying I am going to have ten children, they are going to look after me."

"Today, as with so much in African society, times are changing, and in the extended family's treatment of the elderly, radically so. The growing influence of Western-styled education, free market economics, and accelerated rural to urban migration has placed Africa's traditional extended family under tremendous strain and people's ability and in many cases their willingness to care for the elderly in jeopardy. With swelling numbers of young Ghanaians turning to American style Christian evangelical churches, the worship of the ancestors has lost ground, and thus the intermediaries, the elderly, are no longer very important. Their knowledge of traditional culture has little place in a world where the ability to earn fast money has become the only skill worth cultivating."

Before leaving Ghana, I went to revisit the slave castle Elmina. I sat there listening to the silence of the waves gently dancing with the African night which seemed toiled in time and laughing at eternity. Looking through the doors of no return, the slave fort sat and looked back at me like an immense battled-scarred monument from a bygone time. I asked my pressing question out loud. "If only the fort could speak, the ancestors could answer my questions." And yes, they are the silent witnesses that have seen it all. They were there, strong and youthful, hundreds of years ago when the first slaves voyaged from the stench-filled slave cells onto the unforgiving darkness of the Atlantic. They can remember the time when Africa's myriad and sometimes divided ethnic groups were in harmony with each other, and the land blossomed with homegrown technology and confidence. They looked on as the great king Kaya Magha ruled his illustrious empire from this region, creating a sense of stability and prosperity as his citizens traveled up and down the coast trading gold.

For the spirits of these slave forts, what must have been no more than a short flicker of time, their whispering winds felt the earth tremble as the march of transformation collected steam and, under their wise and nurturing presence, the peoples of Africa began their arduous journey towards freedom. Looking out over the sea, I can hear the ancestors gently whisper. "The African in diaspora need not be worried or confused. We've experienced the ebbs and flow of the eternal river of life and death and understood that no condition is permanent. We've known both magnificent beauty and dreadful ugliness. We've come to embrace both the best and worst of history, and realize that Africa is not as vulnerable as it sometimes appears."

I hope that this book has shown that life in Africa is much more varied and multilayered than its cynics often suggest. If you carry away one thought, let it be this. Although Africa's shortcomings are many, so too are the reasons for them. The continent's dilemmas is not its own. They've been magnified because the vast majority of its people have been neglected, mainly by their own leaders but also by the Western powers who chose to make alliances with despots and strong men.

It is my belief that the only true African revolution and renaissance is one in which the people give birth, or rather rebirth, to an optimistic and integral vision of themselves, for themselves, and by themselves. This cannot be the victim Africa so often portrayed by the Western media. The all too familiar path often magnified through stories of fear, corruption, conflict, and famine are certainly not the majority of narratives shown to me.

Like an artist who has to create with a rugged blank canvas rather than a nice smooth surface that I would prefer, I have had to seek the truth through Africa's paradoxical blemishes. As I have endeavored away at the superficial and sometimes feeble outer layer of the continent's more modern history, I have experienced a profound and essential inner core. This journey has allowed me to rediscover a sense of faith and wonder that I associated with Africa growing up as a child. Most importantly, I discovered an almost mystical capacity of its people, culture, mythos, and within myself to survive against tremendous odds.

In the Shadows of the Ancestors

Notes

Chapter One:

William Bascom, "Four Functions of Folklore", in the study of Folklore, ed. Alan Dundes, 245-250 (Englewood Cliffs: Prentice Hall, 1965).

Raymond Prince, Ifa, Yoruba Divination and Sacrifice, Ibadan University Press, Ibadan, 1963

Judith Gleason, Orisha: The Gods of Yorubaland, Atheneum, New York, 1971

A.J. Garvey, The Philosophy and Opinions of Marcus Garvey. Atheneum, New York, 1969

J.S. Mbiti, African Religions and Philosophy (Honeymoon Books, 1969), p.132

Chapter Two:

Leo Africanus. 1550: The History and Description of Africa and the Notable Things Therein Contained. English edition, 1660. Cited in Basil Davidson, ed, The African Past, pg.90 Boston: Little, Brown,1964

Ian Anderson. 1986. "The Original Journalist". Folk Roots, December 1986, 11, 41.

Ali Mazuri, The Africans-A triple Heritage (Boston: Little, Brown, 1986).

Jamie Monson & James Giblin, Maji Maji "Lifting the Fog of War" (African social studies series, 2010.

Nkoma, "A Question of Relevance" P. 63

Richard Rigby, "Out of Control," British Medical Journal, June 3, 1995, p. 1475

Chapter Three:

Anthony Clayton, The Zanzibar Revolution and its Aftermath (London: C. Hurst, 1981)

Richard F. Burton, Zanzibar City, Island, and Coast, Vol.1 (1872, reprint, New York: Johnson reprint Corporation, 1967).

Michael Lofchie, "Party Conflict in Zanzibar," journal of Modern African Studies 1, no.2 (1965)

Roger Yeager, Tanzania: An African Experiment (Boulder: Westview Press.

Chapter Four:

Claude Ake. Democracy and Development in Africa (Washington: The Brookings Institution, 1996), p.15

Kenyan Vice President George Saitoti, speaking at October 17, 1996, launch of AIDs in Kenya: Socio-economic Impact and Policy Implications.

France Fanon, 1967. Black Skin White Masks, New York: Gove Press.

K.B. Hadjor, On Transforming Africa: Discourse with Africa's leaders. Africa World, New Jersey, 1987.

W.J. Moses, The Golden Age of Black Nationalism. Oxford University, London 1978.

Chapter Five:

"African Visionaries Mandela and Museveni to meet," Reuters, Johannesburg, May 25,1997.

J.M. Coetzee: Disgrace, Secker & Warburg, London, 1999

Peter Godwin: Mukiwa, A White Boy in Africa, Macmillan, London 1996.

David Harrison: The White Tribe of Africa, Macmillan South Africa, Johannesburg, 1981.

Nelson Mandela: Long Walk to Freedom, Little, Brown, London 1994.

Ronald Segal: The Black Diaspora, Fabor & Fabor, London, 1995

Allister Sparks: The Mind of South Africa, Mandarin Paperbacks, London, 1991

Desmond Tutu: No future Without Forgiveness, Rider, London, 1999.

Chapter Six:

African Rights, Facing Genocide: The Nuba of Sudan, London, 1995.

Ahmed Abdel Rahman Al-Bashir, "Problems of Settlement of Immigrants and Refugees in Sudanese Society , D.Phil thesis, University of Oxford, 1978

Amnesty International, Sudan: Human Rights Violations in the Context of Civil War, London, 1989

Robert Collins, Disaster in Darfur, African Geopolitics 15-16, Summer-Fall, October 2004

Samantha Power, "Dying in Darfur," The New Yorker, 30 August 2004.

Harir Sharif, "Arab Belt " versus "African Belt" 1994.

Mahmud Ushari and Baldo Suleyman, El Diein Massacre and Slavery in the Sudan, Khartoum, 1987.

Chapter Seven:

African Trailblazer Begins to Falter, "Financial Times Survey (Ghana), July 9, 1996, p.6 & p.8

Kwesi Kafrona, Organization of African Unity: Twenty-five Years on. Essays in Honor of Kwame Nkrumah, Afroworld, 1988, cited in Brown, Africa's Choices, p.2

UNICEF estimates that sub-Saharan Africa would need $2.4 billion above current spending levels to reach universal primary education. See The Cost and Financing of Primary Education. Options for Reform in Sub-Saharan Africa (New York: UNICEF, 1996), p.3

Index

A